THE ELON MUSK METHOD

Business Principles from the World's Most Powerful Entrepreneur

Randy Kirk

Leaders
Press

ISBN 978-1-943386-44-4 (pbk)

ISBN 978-1-943386-43-7 (ebook)

Dedication and Acknowledgements

I am greatly privileged to have a partner in life that is fully invested in my writing, willing to take a serious interest in the subject matter and is my constant encourager and willing facilitator wherever she is needed. I dedicate this book to my best friend and wife, Toni Kirk.

The book would not have been nearly as readable, but for the outstanding editing of Dr. Toni Kirk, English professor at California Baptist University. How delightful it is for an author to have his editor just a few steps away.

I am deeply indebted to <u>Alinka Rutkowska</u> as my mentor in the development and marketing of this book. She has been an amazing guide who has shown me the important methods for maximizing the potential of this book in the current, Amazon dominated, marketplace.

Why do so many companies fail?

Why are so many owners stuck with low income and ROI?
What would it take to turn most of these companies around?

Doing the Hard Things

Discover the 29 things you should be doing to increase your income and
skyrocket your success!

This eBook is not available for purchase, go to authorremake.com/hard-things
to get this exclusive guide now.

Foreword by Jim Cantrell – founding member of SpaceX

My cell phone rang late on a Friday in July, 2001. The caller on the other end of the line had an unusual accent, somehow faintly British but not entirely. The caller claimed to be an "internet billionaire" and had some vague notions about space missions using private funding. The private funding would be his own net worth. He called me because he was told that I was the right person to talk to who knew about Mars missions and Russian rockets. This "stranger" found me like a proverbial needle in the haystack out of an immense sea of humanity, hoping that we had similar interests and that I could be of assistance to him. The "stranger" was no less than Elon Musk.

At the time, it seemed like a typical phone call. 'Someone with big dreams of flying missions in space and little experience at doing it who was willing to pay to learn the ropes. The phone call from Elon frankly reminded me of a lot of the wealthy characters I occasionally met at the race track who took an interest in road racing. They would show up at the race track to absorb the energy of the undertaking and imagine themselves out competing in fender-to-fender competitions with the other drivers. Some of these wealthy would-be-racers would try it out only to find that this was hard and gritty work with only a questionable return in terms of pleasure and satisfaction. Very few became good enough at the sport to become competitive professionals like Paul Newman, Steve McQueen and Pat Dempsey. Elon was this guy, but this was the space business. In this same sense, the space business is the similar to racing except space machinery is more expensive and our small clique of arrogant insiders are generally better educated and have clean fingernails.

Elon's ideas were big. In fact, they were very big. Initially I had no idea how big his ideas really were as he was deliberately modest in his explanation of intent. His initial approach to me involved "doing something that would prove mankind could become a multi planetary species." Somehow, this necessarily involved something going to Mars, and anything going to Mars needed big rockets, which were very expensive in the western world. This was still in the day that deep space flight was the sole domain of nation states, and the rockets were direct descendants of ICBMs. Big ideas, however, were certainly nothing new and lots of successful internet entrepreneurs were coming out of the woodwork with ideas about making money in space or simply making a mark in history.

I have met a lot of people with big ideas over the years, and some of them even had the money to make these ideas happen. I often listened politely to such ideas with a modest skepticism hidden deeply in my pocket. Some of the ideas are completely crazy, and a self-respecting engineer or scientist would not want to be associated with them. Yet other ideas are modest at first glance but have an underlying truth and brilliance that makes the idea more significant with time. And then there are those ideas that are so audacious that they take your breath away. Elon's ideas were of the latter variety as time has shown. Little did I understand at the time how significant Elon's ideas and actions would truly be later in life.

Elon was different. You could sense it just from the way he framed the problem and the way he logically broke down the solution from first principles. I was not used to this kind of thinking coming from the internet billionaire world. More typically, these folks would have a pet idea that they had been nurturing for many years and secretly wanted to pursue instead of the one that was making them money. In many cases, there was good reason that these ideas were being hidden away from public view.

For those of us who helped Elon in the early days in his space career, our ideas and efforts seemed inconsequential at the time. Elon's vision appeared to those of us who had been in the business as just one more idea that would slowly fade away into the dustbins of history. Little did we understand what this effort would lead to and what bowling pins of history would tumble as a result.

It's truly difficult to overstate how profoundly insignificant these events seemed to all of us at the time. We all understood that Elon was wealthy and that he had plenty of intelligence, motivation, and experience building companies. We all completely failed to appreciate how significant this man was and how this would play out in the future of human exploration. Despite this, Elon remained quietly and supremely confident in his vision. I saw this early on and was not sure how to deal with it. Elon saw something that none of us saw, and there was little that would deter this man from achieving his vision.

There have been a number of works on Elon and the secrets of his life and approach to problem solving. *The Elon Musk Method* is unique in that it gathers up a lot of the early influencers in Elon's circles as he attacked first the banking industry, then the space industry, then automobiles and moved along to power and transportation infrastructures. Randy captures the essence of what drives Elon, and this gives us valuable insight into what has become one of the most influential people of our time.

Jim Cantrell is a serial entreprenuer, race car driver, engineer, and founder of Vector Launch. His career spans over 30 years in aerospace and competition engineering fields. He has worked with many of the most influential people in the space exploration business, from Elon Musk to Carl Sagan. Jim Cantrell has a new book in the works with expected publication in early 2020: *Breaking All The Rules: The Inside Story Of The New Race To Space.*

Contents

Introduction

In an era devoid of living heroes, we have resorted to inventing them for our various screens. Ball players have been humanized by the press. Besides, they don't have any allegiance to their city anymore. Rock stars and movie idols are a dime a dozen with 1000 channels to choose from.

Into the void comes a South African transplant by way of Canada who has now made West Los Angeles his base. He's a nerd who became a rocket scientist by reading up on it. His goal in life is to create a colony on Mars. In order to afford that trip, he's resurrected the failing electric car industry by creating an electric car that has a 2-year waiting list for delivery. He's become by far the largest supplier of rockets for launching commercial satellites, even including national governments like the US and Russia, and he's developing methods for taking city traffic underground. In fact:

> *Ironman director, Jon Favreau, and its star, Robert Downey Jr., were developing the Tony Stark character for the Iron Man film, when Robert Downey Jr. suggested that they meet Elon Musk. Favreau said, "Elon Musk makes no sense — and that's the reason I know him. When I was trying to bring the character of genius billionaire Tony Stark to the big screen in Iron Man, I had no idea how to make him seem real. Robert Downey Jr. said, 'We need to sit down with Elon Musk.' " After the meeting, they decided to use Elon Musk as "inspiration" in their portrayal of Tony Stark on screen. And for Iron Man 2, the Tesla CEO also made an on-screen cameo appearance and allowed some of the filming to occur at SpaceX.*
> - <u>Jon Favreau discusses Elon Musk, Iron Man, and his Tesla</u>

Did Elon Musk ingest some potion, survive a major electrical event, or as many suspect, come from another planet? It is impossible to know for sure, but his string of inventions is outstripping mere mortals like Edison, Ford, Gates, and Jobs. Many forget that his second huge paycheck was from the sale of PayPal, which gave him the seed money to start SpaceX, SolarCity, and Tesla. He had earlier sold an online mapping company for $340 million. (His share $22,000,000.).

Here is the scorecard so far. Keep in mind that Musk is only 47. His best ideas may be still ahead. The following list is in order of contributions by those you are least likely to know about.

- Recently dropped off a panel, Open AI, he cofounded to make sure that artificial intelligence doesn't get out of control by allowing the created to destroy the creators.

- Has an okay from the US government to create the Starlink array of 12,000 satellites that will increase internet speeds, lower costs, and provide internet to everyone on earth. The test units are already in orbit.

- Founded Neuralink, a company whose plan is to hack the human brain and connect it directly to the digital world. This is not a joke.

- Founded the Boring Company to drill tunnels for underground transportation. The Boring Company has contracts for several small projects, including Downtown Chicago to O'Hare airport.

- Invented the hyperloop, then made everything about the project open source. Three companies are now working on full-scale projects to move freight and people at projected speeds of 700 mph over land.

- Conceived Solar City, then merged it into Tesla. Now offering integrated roofs with no visible panels.

- Tesla Energy offers the most dense battery packs available today, completely changing the economics of solar and wind as a reliable energy source.

- Created the autonomous car and truck business. No one was talking about 100% self-driving cars and trucks until Musk said he'd offer just that by 2019. Now every car maker is working on autonomous cars, with many being tested on the road.

- Made the first ever rocket that lands vertically on earth, thereby making all the major components reusable. Reduces cost to launch satellites from $420 million to $80 million per launch.

- Then there's the Tesla line of automobiles and trucks. But you'd have to have been in a coma for the last 10 years not to know about Tesla.

You be the judge. He claims that a combination of curiosity, massive amounts of reading, and working 100 hours a week, every week, accounts for his success. He pretends to be human with all kinds of personal issues dogging him. But is that just a ruse? The real question is whether and when he might be willing to share the real story and then share some of the elixir with us.

Well, I'm no Elon Musk, and my best guess is that you aren't either. But that in no way means that we can't take great lessons away from his approach and apply it to our businesses and our methods of selling, managing, and creating. This book is not just for the owners, but also for anyone in business who wants to be more successful.

Allow me to give you a warning. I'm going to use examples of my own businesses, ideas, and clients in this book. In comparison to what Musk has done, they are very small indeed. However, this difference goes to the heart of the idea. You and I may not have any thoughts about changing the world, but if we dream our own dreams about changing a small part of it and then do something about it, that is going to help us become successful in every possible way that you define success.

Also note that I have used Musk's own words whenever possible. In addition to everything else, he is happy to share the ideas, methods, and philosophies that contribute to his success. I have combed every possible public utterance Musk has made, as well as hundreds of commentaries about Musk, to arrive at the conclusions in this book.

Before we delve into the details, however, it might be useful to define entrepreneur. Webster gives the broadest possible meaning, making entrepreneur synonymous with business owner: "one who organizes, manages, and assumes the risks of a business or enterprise." I would agree that many, maybe even most, Americans would be fine with this definition, but then why have two terms – "entrepreneur" and "business owner" – for exactly the same thing.

Allow me to propose that there are at least five kinds of business owners, and many of these fall into the kind of business owner that Elon Musk exemplifies, the visionary. Here are the five types.

Five types of business owners

1. Practitioners – Many business owners are skilled at a profession or craft which can be used as the basis for being in business. This might be as specific as a divorce attorney or plastic surgeon, or as broad as a retailer who sells and services a product category. Many bakeries, bike shops, fast food places, hair salons, and even sales reps fall into this group. They provide a valuable skill which can be sold through a business. They do take risks. They do establish and manage a company.

2. Managers – Some business owners would be successful owning almost any kind of business. They are excellent at evaluating opportunities, creating plans, managing people and operations, and have great discipline. Many second-generation businesses are run by managers. Franchises and multi-level businesses are suited to managers. This type of person commonly buys an existing business. Managers commonly create very profitable businesses that do well during all types of economic conditions.

3. Trend spotters – These business owners have a profound sense of what is fashionable. This skill is not confined to the products or services they sell, but includes the branding of the enterprise, the look of the physical store, and the management methods. Restaurants are commonly a great example, as are the obvious categories such as clothing stores or exotic health enterprises.

4. Sales professionals – Some folks can sell almost anything to anybody. Give them the pitch and turn them loose. You will find these owners in jewelry stores, bed businesses, and other high-end situations.

5. Visionaries – While it is possible that any of the above could also fit into the following narrower definition of entrepreneur, most do not. They are very good at being a practitioner, manager, trend spotter, or sales professional, but they don't behave as follows:

Visionaries generally invent their own business based on what they see as a perceived need in the market place. They then invent or modify existing products and/or services in such a way to differentiate themselves from the pack. They have no interest in copying other business models, products, services, or even management approaches, though many are forced to conform in some areas lest they risk losing the opportunity to survive long enough to prove their suppositions.

Many talk about these folks as always chasing after the next bright, shiny object. Studies show that they get bored when the project reaches the point where it can be managed and scaled. They are happy to let the engineers and managers take over at that point.

Visionaries are risk takers and prognosticators who boldly go where others fear to tread. Their friends, family, and advisors are generally fighting them all the way. All the way, that is, to great triumphs or to huge defeats. You see, these folks would rather fail big than not try.

After reading this definition, you might conclude that you are very happy to be a manager or practitioner. You aren't that interested in creating a new niche, but are mostly interested in helping folks, and creating a decent living for your family while maintaining an independence that isn't possible as an employee. Congratulations. There is no shame in your plan. You are living the American dream, you know yourself well enough to understand what you do well and what you don't do well, and you are likely to be successful professionally and personally. However, every one of the five different business types listed above will benefit from sitting at the knee of Elon Musk. His approaches will improve whatever position you hold in business.

Commonly, the visionary doesn't care very much about money or what money buys. They are charged up by seeing their vision come true and by seeing their employees, associates, suppliers, and family members benefit from their success.

Sixteen Practices of Elon Musk that Every Entrepreneur Can Learn From

Now, we are ready to talk about the specific elements that produce success for the visionary entrepreneur, and we are going to use the public writings and interviews of Elon Musk to ferret out what these elements are in his approach to business.

In his own words: *"Fundamentally, if you don't have a compelling product at a compelling price, you don't have a great company."* There are sixteen of these elements as follows:

1. Curious
2. Observer
3. Expert
4. Analyst
5. Asks Big Questions
6. Rule Breaker
7. Goal Setter
8. Leader
9. Networker
10. Values People
11. Able to Execute
12. Risk Taker
13. Overcomes obstacles
14. Creates Quality
15. Insists on Incremental Improvement
16. Passionate and Persistent

We will be covering these sixteen principles, one chapter at a time. Let's begin by looking at Musk's early life, his accomplishments, and then take a stab at understanding his vision before we look at each of these principles.

Please don't expect impartial reporting in this book. I am a fan, plain and simple. Full disclosure – as I write this book, I have a small amount of money invested in Tesla. However, my fan status doesn't change the reality that by employing Musk's methods, you are likely to achieve more success in your business and in your life.

Chapter 1 –
The Early Years

Unless there is a massive cover up, Elon Reeve Musk was born. He did not arrive by a rocket from a distant planet, though he might have preferred such a start in life. Nor is there any evidence of a spider bite in the public record.

His arrival on June 28, 1971 in Pretoria, South Africa did not create headlines. But it can be said that his parents, Errol and Maye, provided him with a huge jump start in life. Both his nature and nurture would be solidly positive, at least for the first nine years of his life.

Elon's father, Errol Musk, is an electromechanical engineer, pilot, and sailor, who made a fortune in construction and emerald mining. However, he is described by Elon Musk and other members of his family as a horrible person. While the details are not discussed by the family, Elon says that there was no physical abuse, but he implies emotional abuse and suggests that Errol's business practices were unsavory in the extreme. Elon chose to distance himself from his dad, when he found out that his father had engaged in relations with his step daughter resulting in a child.

So, on one hand, Musk benefited from his father's high IQ, and his substantial financial support during Elon's childhood. Moreover, Errol was an adventurer who owned his own plane, so Elon would see the world and be a part of some of those adventures, including treks deep into the jungles of Africa.

The other provider of Elon's DNA is also very successful. Maye Musk is a dietician and nutritionist with advanced degrees who currently runs her own firm and is in demand as a speaker. Her intellectual prowess is matched by her beauty. She has also continued her 50-year career as a model into her 70's and was recently named spokesperson for Cover Girl.

Maye describes her son as being very precocious as a young child, while Elon describes himself as shy and introverted. Although he devoured books, and his curiosity was insatiable, his time in grammar school was lonely because he admits that he was a know-it-all who had few friends. To make matters worse, he was never athletic, so he didn't fit in with the cool kids who revered athletic ability.

> *"Where a lot of people would go to a great party and have a great time and drink and talk about all sorts of things like rugby or sport, you would find Elon had found the person's library and was going through their books," Musk's dad, electronics engineer Errol Musk, said.* – Business Insider

Divorce is always life altering, and almost universally to the detriment of the children. When Errol and Maye divorced, everything changed for the Musk children. Elon and his younger brother and sister, Kimble and Tosca, lived with Maye and visited Errol. But Elon felt that his dad was lonely and made what he now describes as a mistake. He chose to live with his father, and Kimble joined him.

The teen years were difficult for Elon Musk. He was not a good student, mostly due to boredom, and he was bullied mercilessly by one of the "gangs" at his school who eventually seriously assaulted him physically. As mentioned, his father was emotionally abusive.

When he grew into the tall, substantial man that he is today and took some self-defense classes, the bullying stopped.

Overall, those who knew him during this period saw absolutely no evidence of the brilliant career that was to come. There are, however, three hints that might have given a careful observer a reason to expect greatness. Musk was very interested in electronics and saw that a local electronics retailer was stocking a few early computers. He bugged Errol to buy him one, and soon he was the proud owner of a Commodore VIC-20.

"It was supposed to take like six months to get through all the lessons, Elan said. "I just got super OCD on it and stayed up for three days with no sleep and did the entire thing. It seemed like the most super compelling thing I had ever seen." From Elon Musk: Tesla, SpaceX, and the Quest for a Fantastic Future

Musk's passion for his new computer resulted in his learning to code, which led to his creation of Blaster, a video game he created at age 12. An explainer for the game notes that "In this game, you have to destroy an alien space freighter, which is carrying deadly hydrogen bombs and status beam machines. This game makes good use of sprites and animation, and in this sense, makes the listing worth reading."

In 1984, South African publication *PC and Office Technology* published the source code to the game, which required 167 lines of instructions to run. The magazine paid the young Musk $500 for his work. You can play an online version of the game even now by going to http://blastar-1984.appspot.com/

The second hint of Musk's future success was his many small entrepreneurial efforts, culminating in his attempt to open a video arcade before he was 18.

The third hint would be his early adoption (in his middle teens) of a world view that would set the stage for his future in clear terms. Musk speaks often of two books that have been a source for this worldview, including Isaac Asimov's *Foundation* series, which tells the work of Hari Seldon, who invents a method of predicting the future based on crowd behavior. Seldon predicts a 30,000-year Dark Ages and creates a plan to save mankind by creating colonies of humans on other planets. Sound familiar?

"Asimov certainly was influential because he was seriously paralleling Gibbon's Decline and Fall of the Roman Empire, but he applied that to a sort of modern galactic empire," Musk explains. "The lesson I drew from that is you should try to take the set of actions that are likely to prolong civilization, minimize the probability of a dark age and reduce the length of a dark age if there is one." Rolling Stone Interview

The second book of influence was *The Hitchhiker's Guide to the Galaxy*, by Douglas Adams.

> *I guess when I was around 12 or 15…I had an existential crisis, and I was reading various books on trying to figure out the meaning of life and what does it all mean? It all seemed quite meaningless and then we happened to have some books by Nietzsche and Schopenhauer in the house, which you should* not *read at age 14 (laughter). It is bad, it's really negative. So then I read* Hitchhikers Guide to the Galaxy *which is quite positive I think and it highlighted an important point which is that a lot of times the question is harder than the answer. And if you can properly phrase the question, then the answer is the easy part. So, to the degree that we can better understand the universe, then we can better know what questions to ask. Then whatever the question is that most approximates: what's the meaning of life? That's the question we can ultimately get closer to understanding. And so I thought to the degree that we can expand the scope and scale of consciousness and knowledge, then that would be a good thing." -* FreshDialogues.com 2013

So, by the middle teens, Musk had arrived at two conclusions about his future; … **"*try to take the set of actions that are likely to prolong civilization, minimize the probability of a dark age and reduce the length of a dark age if there is one,*"** and **"*to the degree that we can expand the scope and scale of consciousness and knowledge, then that would be a good thing.*"**

This short biography of Elon Musk's childhood is only intended to provide insight into his later accomplishments. If you would like to read an amazing and detailed version, Ashlee Vance has created a thrilling adventure biography, *Elon Musk: Tesla, SpaceX, and the Quest for a Fantastic Future.*

Chapter 2 –
The Accomplishments

Elon Musk wanted very much to go to America. He had traveled widely and come to the conclusion that his greatest opportunity lay in California.

> *"Whenever I'd read about cool technology, it'd tend to be in the United States or, more broadly, North America. [...] I kind of wanted to be where the cutting edge of technology was, and of course within the United States, Silicon Valley is where the heart of things is. Although, at the time, I didn't know where Silicon Valley was. It sounded like some mythical place."* – <u>Fresh Dialogues</u>

Maye Musk was born in Canada, so Elon saw his opportunity to reach the US through his mother's citizenship in Canada. Against his father's wishes and with little cash reserve, he moved to Canada and a very uncertain immediate future. He had relatives there, but no clear idea about where he would live or what he would do to make a living.

Taking on various odd jobs, including cleaning out boiler rooms or cutting logs with a chainsaw, Musk built up his cash and established himself. Then, still just 18 years old, he enrolled at Queen's University in Kingston, Ontario. After two years, Musk transferred to the University of Pennsylvania, having been granted a scholarship.

Eventually Musk earned an economics degree from Wharton School and BS in physics from the College of Arts and Science. He was accepted into the Ph.D. program in applied physics at Stanford, but he dropped out after two days, seeing an opportunity he fears would be gone if he doesn't take advantage. He theorized that he could always go back and get the degree.

While in College, Musk started to move out of his shell. Shy to this day, he never lacks boldness, and this is the attribute that others start to notice. He says that he purposely shut down the know-it-all part of his personality, and purposely started to work on his presence, even competing in public speaking competitions. His employers, school associates, and friends started to describe Musk as having an intensity that "separates him from the rest of humanity."

In the following pages we will take a look at the specific companies that he has started and the current status of each. Included will be:

Zip2. – Online business to consumer advertising similar to Yelp today.
X.com – Online peer-to-peer money transfers which became Paypal
SpaceX – Rocket manufacturing and payload transportation to space
Starlink – Satellite array designed to provide fast Internet service worldwide
Tesla – Autonomous electric automobile manufacturing
Tesla Energy – Battery manufacturing for cars, homes, and utilities
Solar City – Solar panel and roof manufacturing and installation
Open AI – Non-profit working to keep artificial intelligence from destroying mankind
Neurolink – Developing methods for computers to directly link with the human brain
Hyperloop – High speed transportation using magnetic elevation and vacuum tubes
The Boring Company – Tunnel drilling for underground transportation and utilities

Zip2

It's 1995. The Internet is barely a year old. Small businesses had no idea how to benefit. In fact, ten years later fewer than 50% of small businesses had a presence on the internet. Elon and brother Kimble see an opening. They created Zip2, which today can be best explained as a kind of primitive version of today's Yelp.com or GoogleMyBusiness.com.

The idea was to provide consumers with a way to find a local business based on business category and location. But there was one rub. How do you get those businesses to pay for the advertising if consumers aren't using the web yet, and/or how do you get the consumers to use the web to find a business if their experience results in few, if any, potential businesses in the search results? The young company was facing the classic chicken and egg problem.

The Musk brothers found the solution that others failed to see. Newspapers and phone books were going to be the big loser in the Internet revolution. If consumers could find the local bakery on the Internet, why would the bakery buy ads in the newspaper or the phone book. So Kimble started convincing the newspapers that they need to get ahead of the curve by shifting their sales effort to the Internet, using the Zip2 engine.

Elon, meanwhile, is doing the coding. Maybe the Musk brothers knew this going in, or maybe they didn't, but they were biting off a huge endeavor, and their meager startup capital was not going to last long.

By point of reference, in 1995, my partner and I started BicycleMall. com. Similar to Zip2, we hoped to send consumers to BicycleMall to find products and then be sent to a local shop to make the purchase. Like Zip2, we were going to get the manufacturers to pay for the advertising of their products. Unlike Zip 2, we had to pay for the coding of this new idea, but $100,000 later (in 1995 dollars) we threw in the towel.

Even with Elon doing the coding, he and Kimble were constantly on the verge of failure, primarily due to cash constraints. Elon was living in the office and showering at the YMCA. The story of their survival makes great reading. See *Elon Musk: Tesla, SpaceX, and the Quest for a Fantastic Future*

In early 1996, Mohr Davidson Ventures invested $3 million into Zip2. This allowed the company to switch their immediate emphasis from local to national and to concentrate on newspapers as the paying customer. They also brought in some experienced coders, streamlining the software dramatically.

The early success of Zip2 gave Musk another shot in the arm of self-confidence, which led to him becoming much more assertive. As will be noted later, this assertiveness is a huge blessing, but it can be a curse.

CitiSearch was a major competitor with much the same vision as Zip2. In 1998, the two companies were on the verge of a merger, but negotiations soured, and the deal was not completed. But then in February 1999, Compaq Computer offered a cash deal of $307 million. In less than 5 years, Musk had earned himself a paycheck for $22,000,000, and set himself up for life at age 28. But unlike other dotcom winners, Musk had a new company in mind even before Zip2 was sold.

X.com

Musk's long-term vision would have to wait. While you could make a case that Zip2 and X.com helped people, they did little to keep the world out of a new Dark Age. It would be fair to say that Musk was taking advantage of opportunities that could both provide him with a living and make use of his entrepreneurial drive and energy.

Musk had worked in a bank for a while and had a keen interest in the way banks operated. He believed that bankers were too lazy to see that there was a big opportunity to open an online bank. While the coding for this idea might have been easier than the coding to create Zip2, the regulatory hurdles associated with creating a bank were immense. Even after investing $10M of his $22M in X.com, the company needed more funds.

In addition to the regulatory issues, there was another chicken and egg problem. The entry point for X.com was free, peer-to-peer and/or consumer-to-business payments. But if I want to pay you for babysitting my kids and you aren't online with X.com, the transaction doesn't happen, and I'm discouraged and consequently unlikely to try to use it again. What to do?

After a venture capital infusion, Musk decided to literally pay consumers to join. The first month X.com gave new members $20 in free online cash just to join. This was hugely successful. The second month, they lowered the free cash offer to $10, and in the third month, lowered it again to $5. The idea worked, but X.com quickly burned through $60,000,000 in cash.

Meanwhile another startup had the same idea. Confinity (aka PayPal) was in a race with X.com to acquire customers. In those days, the Internet's startups asserted that whoever was fastest to establish the concept would ultimately take huge amounts of the market share.

In this case, both companies were starting to exhaust their cash resources in the fight to be #1. After just one year in business, Confinity merged with X.com, and Musk was ousted from his CEO spot due to conflicts in vision. Musk still wanted a bank. The winning block of shareholders were satisfied to continue on the conservative path by offering peer-to-peer payments.

Then, in October of 2002, eBay purchased PayPal for $1.5 billion. In just over 3 years Musk had turned his $22 million into $165 million after taxes.

SpaceX

After being ousted from the CEO position at PayPal, Musk lost no time in turning his attention to his big plan…getting to Mars.

With so much money at his disposal, Musk could afford to spend liberally to make his point about the importance of humans continuing to explore space. He was unhappy that the US had basically given up on efforts to explore other planets. So, with no intent to make money, he decided to blow a huge amount of money on a symbolic gesture. He would find a way to send a small greenhouse garden to Mars. The details are unimportant, but his initial goal was to inspire new interest in interplanetary exploration. Camera's would be positioned to send back photos of this little oasis against the red soil background. This early idea gives a glimpse into the promotional side of Musk. This is the same Musk who would send his Tesla Roadster into deep space with pictures of the red space car beamed back to earth.

Famously, Musk starts the Mars quest by attempting to buy some used ICBM's from Russia.

Jim Cantrell, an actual rocket scientist, was one of the early cadres advising Musk regarding his space ambitions. He tells the story this way:

> *There's more to the story than simply wandering around Russia. Elon came to me in 2001 wanting to "do something that could demonstrate that humanity can become a multi planetary species." He still uses that phrase. He wanted to do it with his own money and had the idea of launching a colony of mice to Mars. He contacted me specifically*

because I was a well-known Soviet expert, have experience launching satellites from Russia, I speak Russian, I know the Russian industry from my work on the French/Soviet Mars 94 program, and I spent a sum total of two years there in the 1990's working DoD programs. He knew that he could only afford a Russian rocket with his budget and this is where he started. Some shades of the motivations to start SpaceX to come later. For Elon, I was the best starting point because of my experience and knowledge of the Russian aerospace industry and Mars landers.

I gathered a group of people in the US to study this mission and we eventually came up with the idea to land a plant growth chamber on Mars to show that life could thrive on Mars. I led the study supported by John Garvey, Chris Thompson, Bob Zubrin, Jim French, Mike Griffin, Tomas Svitek, Tom Mueller, Taber MacCallum, Jane Poynter and Dave Bearden. It was called Mars Oasis. We identified the Dnepr launch vehicle as the best choice for the mission to be launched in 2006 if I remember correctly. We went to Russia three times: once to talk to Lavotchkin about building our lander (thought to be cheaper than doing it in the US), another time to talk to a number of launch vehicle providers and the last time to actually purchase two Dnepr launches. When they refused to negotiate, Elon decided to build the rocket himself - the modern Falcon 9. Jim Cantrell in a Quora answer. Nov 25, 2015*

After two trips, this door is closed. The Russians don't seem overly enthusiastic about the opportunity, and the asking price of $8M seems too high for Musk.

In an early use of the idea of first principles (discussed in detail later in this book), Musk computes the raw material cost of these rockets and realizes that he can build new ones for much less than buying the old, out of date, Russian units. Moreover, why send the little greenhouse. He decides to start a business that can offer cheaper trips to space for the countries, universities, and businesses that needed transportation for their satellites.

Musk now says: "I gave basically both SpaceX and Tesla from the beginning a probability of less than 10 percent likelihood to succeed," and "If you were to do a risk-adjusted rate of return estimate on various industry opportunities, I would put building rockets and cars pretty close to the bottom of the list. They would have to be the dumbest things to do." - <u>CNBC</u>

On the other hand, if SpaceX can successfully drop the cost of getting items into orbit, or to the International Space Station, or to other planets, there are huge lists of potential customers who could use the services who can't profitably use them at the 2001 price tag.

The company is started almost entirely from Musk's new fortune. He eventually sinks $100 million of his own funds into the venture. As of December, 2018, SpaceX is valued at $30.5 billion, and is launching more rockets and tonnage per year than has ever been done by any company or sovereign nation in the past.

How is that possible? Musk threw out the playbook. The aerospace companies and the governments that supported their efforts had unlimited budgets and very specific goals to achieve. Musk saw things the other way around. How can we safely get satellites into orbit at the lowest possible cost, whatever the payload is?

This meant rethinking every aspect of how rockets are built; how, when, and where they were launched; and what would happen if the parts could be reused rather than discarded after every flight. The result is a lowering of the cost per flight from over $1 billion for NASA to a current $65 million for SpaceX, and some expectation of a cost as low as $7 million when reusing all the parts that are discarded by every other space endeavor.

Of course, when competition enters into the business, others will try to find a way to meet or beat the price, quality, or performance. Boeing, Bigelow Airspace, Blue Origin, Virgin Galactic Vector Launch, Lockheed Martin, Rocket Lab, Russia, and China are working to bring their costs down, as well.

Musk still insists all of the SpaceX work is dedicated to a final goal of populating Mars. He will start testing a newly designed and named "Starship" in early 2019. The earlier version of this rocket was called the

BFR, and it is already the most powerful rocket in use today. The goal is to send the first Starship to Mars in 2022, loaded with supplies that will be needed when humans are sent in 2024.

Starlink

The age of cable is likely over. So too, we may be nearing the end of cell towers. Several companies are creating satellite arrays designed to provide Internet service from space rather than using current methods. Musk believes that his massive deployment will be the eventual winner in this race to create high speed connectivity.

> *I don't talk that much about StarLink, but essentially, it's intended to provide low latency, high bandwidth Internet connectivity throughout the world. That actually will not be enough cognitive processing power onboard the satellite system, in any way, to be a Skynet thing.* – Spaceship.com

As the project now stands, Musk intends to send some 12,000 communication satellites into an orbit pattern that has been approved by US regulators. Musk estimates that the total cost to deploy Starlink will be $10 billion. Some of this will come from SpaceX profits, but in December of 2018, SpaceX sold $500 million in stock specifically earmarked for Starlink.

When completed, the constellation of satellites will reach every remote place on Earth and will provide very high bandwidth. There are two operating test satellites already in use, and SpaceX reports that you can play games requiring the greatest bandwidth with no latency.

SpaceX has stated that the value of this system will be greater than the value of the rest of SpaceX.

Tesla – Electric Automobiles

With so little to do in building and running a rocket company (really?), Musk, like the typical visionary entrepreneur, invests in a startup with his leftover time and energy. (Warning: this is for audacious, visionary entrepreneurs. Don't try this at home.)

Martin Eberhard and Mark Tarpenning were the founders of Tesla Motors. They were working on an electric powered roadster but needed venture capital money.

> *Back in 2001, Tarpenning, being a bit of a space nerd, had dragged Eberhard along to see a PayPal cofounder <u>speak at a Mars Society conference held at Stanford.</u> His name was Elon Musk, and his ideas about what to do in the space industry were strikingly clear. Tarpenning and Eberhard introduced themselves.* – <u>Business Insider</u>

Eberhard sends Musk an email:

> *"We would love to talk to you about Tesla Motors," he wrote, "particularly if you might be interested in investing in the company. I believe that you have driven AC Propulsion's tzero car. If so, you already know that a high-performance electric car can be made. We would like to convince you that we can do so profitably, creating a company with very high potential for growth, and at the same time breaking the compromise between driving performance and efficiency."*

> *Musk replied that evening.*

> *"Sure," he said. "Friday this week or Friday next week would work."*
> – <u>Business Insider</u>

Musk has been interested in saving the planet from global warming through the adoption of sustainable energy since College, so he sinks $10 million into this little company and helps out with engineering and design. He also becomes chairman of the board.

By 2007, Tesla had a working product, had created quite a fuss, and had orders to build more. Unfortunately, the co-founder and CEO was in over his head. Musk took over leadership just as the economy was tanking and the major auto companies were headed for bankruptcy due to the great recession. But Musk was determined to create an electric car for a very specific purpose that had nothing to do with profit. He stated that since he had already put $55 million into the company, he might as well take over the wheel. He becomes CEO.

When asked by Leslie Stahl on 60 Minutes about competition from GM and others...

Musk appeared unconcerned.

"If somebody comes and makes a better electric car than Tesla, and it's so much better than ours that we can't sell our cars and we go bankrupt, I still think that's a good thing for the world." Space?

"The whole point of Tesla is to accelerate the advent of electric vehicles and sustainable transport," he said. *"We're trying to help the environment, we think it's the most serious problem that humanity faces."*

On September 28, 2008, Musk had his fortune on the line. SpaceX had endured three failures in row and had only enough money to try one last time. This was that day. Meanwhile Musk had plowed the rest of his $160 million PayPal money into Tesla, some $70 million. And as the fate of SpaceX was being determined on that day, Tesla was also on the verge of failure. In fact, if funds weren't added by the end of 2008, the company would have to shut down.

We came very close to both companies not succeeding in 2008. We had three failures of the SpaceX rocket, so we were 0 for 3. We had the crazy financial recession, the Great Recession. The Tesla financing round was falling apart because it's pretty hard to raise money for a startup car company if GM and Chrysler are going bankrupt. [...] Fortunately, at the end of 2008, the fourth launch, which was the last launch we had money for, worked for SpaceX, and we closed the Tesla financing round Christmas Eve 2008, the last hour of the last day that it was possible." Elon Musk

Since 2008, Tesla has sold 500,000 cars, with a goal to sell 1,000,000 per year. So far, the company has models S 3 X with the introduction of the Y (which spells?) expected very soon. He has taken orders for Semitrucks and a pickup is in the works.

The real goal is the same as it was when he invested. He wants to force the major car companies to get serious about shifting to electric. And he seems to have succeeded in that quest! Mercedes, GM, Ford, Volkswagon,

Porche, Jaguar, Volvo, Audi, BMW, Nissan and Hyundai are all investing billions in electric.

> *"Probably in 10 years, more than a half of new vehicle production is electric in the United States, half of all production will be EV, I think almost all cars produced will be autonomous."* Teslarati, July 17, 2017

Tesla Energy

I have searched the Internet to find the source, but I have come up short. I am quite certain that I read a quote from a major industrialist to the effect: Whoever invents a better battery will be the richest person on earth. (Here are some articles you might enjoy that almost reach that conclusion: "The Great Battery Race": https://foreignpolicy.com/2010/10/12/the-great-battery-race/ or "The Race to Build the Better Battery That the World Desperately Needs: https://www.vox.com/2015/2/22/8084703/powerhouse-steve-levine-review.)

Now I will add to this idea: the battery is the key to the Tesla machine; not the car, not the solar panels; but the battery. *At the Q2 analyst call, Tesla management had re-affirmed that it expects* **energy storage revenue to equal that of autos** *for the company*, according to Seeking Alpha. This is a little reported fact that is huge in its implications.

> *"Without decisive action to lay the groundwork today, the massive volume of affordable, high efficiency panels needed for unsubsidized solar power to out compete fossil fuel grid power simply will not be there when it is needed,"*- Elon Musk

By 2025 16% - 25% of all new cars sold will be fully electric, according to multiple sources. Musk believes it will be 50% by 2028. Thirty different electric car models have been announced as being currently at some phase of development, with most being offered for sale by 2020. Somebody is going to be supplying the batteries for five million or more cars per year in 2025 and increasing each year after that. No one is better positioned to be a major producer of these batteries than Tesla.

In addition to the batteries, Tesla intends to eventually offer the entire power train to those who wish to use Tesla parts as the foundation of their vehicles. With three Gigafactories running or under construction and 17 on the drawing board, Tesla could be producing way more than batteries for those millions of cars.

Musk has used Australia as his proving ground to show how the addition of Tesla virtual power plants can dramatically increase the efficacy and efficiency of solar, wind, and other alternative energy generators. Forbes predicts that $620 billion will be spent on such storage in the next 20 years. That may be a low estimate. Musk has stated that the demand for storage batteries is already much greater than the supply and expects the demand to grow exponentially over the next 20 years. He states that the it will take 100 Gigafactories to make the needed batteries, and other sources suggest the number might be closer to 1000.

> *"The rate of stationary storage is going to grow exponentially," Tesla's Elon Musk said at a shareholder meeting earlier this year.*

> *"For many years to come each incremental year will be about as much as all of the preceding years, which is a crazy, crazy growth rate."* - Stockhead

California now requires all new home construction to have solar roofs. Other states and countries are almost certain to add their name to this now short list. Most of those solar roofs will have Tesla Powerwall battery packs, since at the low current cost of $7600, installed the improvement of efficiency in-home use is easy to demonstrate. You store electricity during the night when rates are low, and then use as necessary during the day to supplement solar power when usage is high.

In addition to those applications, you have commercial and government use. It is hard to understand why every government and major commercial consumer of energy is not already converted to solar, but this will happen over the next very few years. What government does not require by fiat, companies and governments will do because of the clear savings in dollars. Industrial and government applications of the Tesla Powerwall will create further demand. The Powerwall can be used with or with-out Solar power. With huge swings in the cost of electricity from the utilities between daytime rates and overnight rates, the batteries can be charged each night and used during peak rate periods.

Tesla is a vertically integrated primary manufacturer of solar generating equipment, battery storage, and electric automobiles. All of these product categories are barely at the beginning of their ramp ups. Musk has said that he just wants to lead the way, forcing other companies to follow. If Tesla successfully enjoys even 10% share of these three industries, it will likely be the largest company on planet Earth (and maybe Mars, too.)

Tesla buys SolarCity

Musk's intention to save the earth included a strong interest in sustainable energy. While he was creating his rocket company, he set up a business with his cousins to work on solar panels.

> *"How do we have a solar roof that's better than a normal roof? A roof that looks better than normal roofs, generates electricity, lasts longer, has better insulation, and has an installed cost that is less than a normal roof plus the cost of electricity."* | Teslarati

> *"People think of Tesla as an eclectic car company but the whole purpose of Tesla was to accelerate the advent of sustainable energy."* | Inverse

The Solar panel and roof division of Tesla, known under the subsidiary name of SolarCity, was not "founded" by Musk. He says that he can't lay claim to the title of founder because he did not put in the requisite sweat equity. However, it was Musk's idea, he provided $10 million in seed capital, and he sat as chairman. The company was run by his cousins, Peter and Lyndon Rive.

Tesla purchased SolarCity in 2016 in order to create a fully integrated new energy company. Musk stated that it was "an accident of history that Tesla and SolarCity were two separate companies."

Since the merger, the residential solar panel portion of SolarCity has been very quiet, though the overall contribution of SolarCity is significant to Tesla. The focus seems to have shifted to the Tesla Solar Roof where the photovoltaic electrical energy generating devices and system would be integrated into the roof surface, and moving away from the more traditional approach of solar panels on an existing roof. Musk said it this way: "It's not a thing on a roof. It is the roof."

"This is really a fundamental part of achieving a differentiated product strategy," Musk said. *"It actually doesn't cannibalize the existing product of putting solar on roof."*

"If your roof is nearing end-of-life, you definitely don't want to put solar panels on it, because you're going to have to replace the roof. So, there is a huge market segment that is currently inaccessible to SolarCity, because people know they're going to have to replace their roof," Musk continued. *"So, why not have a solar roof that's better in many other ways as well. SolarCity CEO Lyndon Rive added that "Just in the U.S. there are 5 million new roofs installed every year and then this is a product we're focused on the—primarily focused on the new roof market."* Solar Reviews

Open AI

Artificial intelligence is taking over, whether we like it or not. Musk is very concerned.

"It's not as though I think the risk is that the AI would develop all on its own right off the bat. The concern is that someone may use it in a way that is bad, and even if they weren't going to use it in a way that is bad, somebody would take it from them and use it in a way that's bad. That, I think, is quite a big danger. We must have democratization of AI technology and make it widely available. That's the reason [we] created OpenAI.

There's a quote that I love from Lord Acton—he was the guy who came up with, 'Power corrupts and absolute power corrupts absolutely'— which is that 'freedom consists of the distribution of power and despotism in its concretion.' I think it's important if we have this incredibly powerful AI that it not be concentrated in the hands of the few." Elon Musk

"Between Facebook, Google and Amazon – and arguably Apple, but they seem to care about privacy – they have more information about you than you can remember," he elaborates to me. *"There's a lot of risk in concentration of power. So, if AGI [artificial general intelligence] represents an extreme level of power, should that be controlled by a few people at Google with no oversight?"* Rolling Stone

Musk is very concerned that artificial intelligence is the most dangerous threat to the future of humankind. The result was that he contributed about $10 million to the non-profit company Open AI. Because of his commercial involvement in the use of AI throughout his various enterprises, including Neuralink, Musk has stepped down from his position on the board.

Neuralink

You undoubtedly have watched the Matrix and other sci fi movies that use computer power to dramatically improve our human abilities. Musk sees an opportunity there:

> *"We're already a cyborg. You have a digital version of yourself or partial version of yourself online in the form of your e-mails and your social media and all the things that you do. And you have, basically, superpowers with your computer and your phone and the applications that are there. You have more power than the president of the United States had 20 years ago. You can answer any question; you can video conference with anyone anywhere; you can send a message to millions of people instantly. You just do incredible things."* Elon Musk

(…and here…)

> *Musk explained that the long-term goal is to achieve "symbiosis with artificial intelligence", which Musk perceives as an existential threat to humanity if it goes unchecked. At present time, some neuroprosthetics can interpret brain signals and allow disabled people to control their prosthetic arms and legs. Musk aims to link that technology with implants that, instead of actuating movement, can interface at broadband speed with other types of external software and gadgets.* – Wikipedia

Reality imitating art. Maybe we will all be able to upload Elon's brain onto our computer, then download the app to our own feeble brain.

Hyperloop

In the summer of 2012, Elon Musk announced that he was working on yet another idea:

Musk is cooking up plans for something he calls the Hyperloop. He won't share specifics but says it's some sort of tube capable of taking someone from downtown San Francisco to Los Angeles in 30 minutes. He calls it a "fifth mode of transportation"—the previous four being train, plane, automobile, and boat.

"What you want is something that never crashes, that's at least twice as fast as a plane, that's solar powered and that leaves right when you arrive, so there is no waiting for a specific departure time," Musk says.

His friends claim he's had a Hyperloop technological breakthrough over the summer. "I'd like to talk to the governor and president about it," Musk continues. "Because the $60 billion bullet train they're proposing in California would be the slowest bullet train in the world at the highest cost per mile. They're going for records in all the wrong ways." The cost of the SF-LA Hyperloop would be in the $6 billion range, he says. - Business Insider 2012

Of course, the bullet train in California is now projected to cost of $77 billion and might have some operation trains by 2025-7, assuming they don't run out of money. The idea is that the train will make the trip in 3.5 hours, better than a car, but three times that of a plane.

Musk unveiled a detailed look at Hyperloop in August of 2013 but noted that he could not develop this idea into a commercial reality due to the pressing requirements for his time at SpaceX and Tesla. He made all of the plans open source and suggested that anyone who might care to create Hyperloops were free to do so.

The Hyperloop concept has come under withering fire from many experts, but two companies are now in the process of attempting to make the first commercial hyperloop segments. For example, Hyperloop Transportation Technologies has just shipped its prototype passenger capsule to a 320 meter test track, where testing will begin in 2019.

The hyperloop name is not trademarked; hence, there is some confusion about what a hyperloop really is. The Boring Company tunnel systems are being called Hyperloop by some in the press. These systems are not anything like the Hyperloop concept, so it is unclear why there is this current confusion.

The Boring Company

We all have our fair share of daily stress producers, and one of the most frustrating aspects of urban life is traffic. When we are faced with problems, we can either deal with them, complain about them, or do something about them. Musk looked at the traffic issue in Los Angeles and started trying to engineer a solution.

> *"The fundamental problem with cities is that we build cities in 3D. You've got these tall buildings with lots of people on each floor, but then you've got roads, which are 2D. That obviously just doesn't work. You're guaranteed to have gridlock. But you can go 3D if you have tunnels. And you can have many tunnels crisscrossing each other with maybe a few meters of vertical distance between them and completely get rid of traffic problems."* Elon Musk

Musk conceived of a system of tunnels under LA that would use some type of automated vehicles to move cars at 150 mph from place to place. Various iterations have been offered, including automated Tesla vehicles, any vehicle on an automated skate, or any automated vehicle with a pair of clamps attached to the front wheels to keep the car on the track. The vehicle then moves under its own power.

A test tunnel has been built and shown to the public in 2018. Various projects are under development. Maybe the most prominent among these is Musk's offer to build a system connecting downtown Chicago with O'Hare airport at no cost to the city, and with a proposed $1 ticket cost.

> *The next goal for The Loop, according to Musk, is a throughput of 4,000 cars per hour at speeds up to 155 mph. Cars would exit future versions of The Loop via exits and off-ramps that deliver vehicles street level. To increase usage, public and shared transportation would be subject to a $1 fare, but private vehicles would pay $4. In a tweet, Musk clarified that pedestrians and cyclists could ride future Loops in dedicated public vehicles.* – Engineering 360

Other transportation projects are planned for Baltimore and Los Angeles. In January 2019 Musk has offered to tunnel <u>through a mountain in Australia</u>, to <u>build sewer and utility tunnels</u>, and most recently to expand the <u>Cern particle accelerator</u>.

On the Drawing Board

At least two other transportation concepts have been offered by Musk. He believes that his rockets could offer city-to-city passenger transportation anywhere on earth in 45-minutes. The rockets would launch and land on specially designed pods that could be land or sea-based.

> *In SpaceX's video that illustrates the idea, passengers take a large boat from a dock in New York City to a floating launchpad out in the water. There, they board the same rocket that Musk wants to use to send humans to Mars by 2024. But instead of heading off to another planet once they leave the Earth's atmosphere, the ship separates and breaks off toward another city — Shanghai.*

> *Just 39 minutes and some 7,000 miles later, the ship reenters the atmosphere and touches down on another floating pad, much like the way SpaceX lands its Falcon 9 rockets at sea. Other routes proposed in the video include Hong Kong to Singapore in 22 minutes, London to Dubai or New York in 29 minutes, and Los Angeles to Toronto in 24 minutes. –* <u>The Verge</u>

Musk also indicates that he has designed a vertical-lift-off electric jet that would also dramatically reduce the time and expense of air travel.

> *The founder of Tesla Motors and Space Exploration Technologies announced that in the near future he may work to develop an all-electric supersonic jet that could take off and land vertically.*

> *Elon Musk said that supersonic air travel, exceeding the speed of sound using an electric-powered jet that could take off and land without the need for a long runway, was the 'ultimate form of transport.'*

> *'If somebody doesn't do that, maybe at some point in the future, I will,' Musk, 42, said during a YouTube video chat with a group of technology entrepreneurs on Thursday.*

Musk said that he wanted to set up a company to build such an aircraft in the future, though he is currently preoccupied with his other projects, including a planned mission to Mars.

Traveling at supersonic speeds, an aircraft could fly from London to Shanghai in about seven and a half hours, which compares with more than 11 hours for a direct commercial flight, according to **Bloomberg***.*

An all-electric plane would benefit the environment, in addition to being fast and quiet, Musk noted. – The Daily Mail

Chapter 3 –
The Vision

Elon Musk received his life's calling when he was a young teen. This is not at all unusual, and I would encourage you to contemplate what you said or felt that you wanted to do with your life when you were between 12 and 15. It might still alter your direction. There is something about the openness of a child age 12 that has yet to be rooted out by peer pressure in middle school that exposes the most powerful inner voice.

Musk simply felt that he should do things that mattered, and that what mattered was keeping the world from entering into another Dark Ages. He later determined that the most likely subject matters for helping the human race avert such a disaster would be found in energy, transportation, the internet, and space.

Through all of my research to date, I do not find any public statement by Musk about his specific motivations for choices made between 18 and 31, though these seem more pragmatic and unrelated to his eventual vision…the schools he attended, the jobs he took, and the first internet companies, Zip2 and X.com…seem like the practical decisions of a young entrepreneur who saw the internet as a huge potential opportunity.

Certainly, at age 31 Musk was in a position to do almost anything he wanted. With $190 million dollars in the bank, he began to focus on the idea that man needed to keep exploring the heavens. He also worried about things like sustainable energy supplies, and the early concerns about global warming. Later he would also become very concerned about the ugly and dangerous potential of artificial intelligence.

We all have the same number of hours in the day, and roughly the same number of years on this planet. Some appear to drift through life without any thought of their purpose. Others contemplate their purpose but never spend the time or take the risks to play it out. Some choose to look for meaning and then act with purpose to maximize their contribution. Elon Musk seems to be emblematic of this third group.

Using his own words and the words of some of his closest associates, here is the Musk vision.

"If you have a great solar roof, and you have a battery pack in your house, and you have an electric car, that scales worldwide. You can solve the whole energy equation with that." - Elon Musk (Oct 28, 2016 | Source)

"…he's a Rogue. He has some very grandiose visions: make "Mankind a multi-planetary species" and "remove humanity's dependence on fossil fuels" to which he applies enormous energy, time and resources. Elon is very intelligent, has a nearly inexhaustible energy, and possesses an incredible appetite for making progress. He is really a Rogue because he does it outside of the normal channels of thinking and outside of the normal channels of doing. He, like many of us who have joined him at various parts of his adventures, simply realized at a point in his life that radical transformation cannot happen within the system but must happen from outside the system. Some of us even believe that the larger economic system and society actually hinders progress and you have to be on the outside of it to truly change things for the better.

Those of us who helped Elon start SpaceX had all self-ejected from Corporate America at one point or another because of its conformity in thinking and limitations on doing. Early SpaceX was a merry band of brothers who were refugees from the oppressive 'group think' of Corporate America - and especially the aerospace industry. To us, it was an archaic economic system frighteningly similar to the Soviet command and control economic system that the Cold War sought to defeat. This kind of environment was not conducive to our sense of what needed to be accomplished to move humanity forward or even to doing things that resulted in a satisfied sense of accomplishment. Those we left behind "in the system" referred to us derisively as "Rogue

Engineers.” We came to wear those words, meant to insult us, as a badge of honor. Elon is the biggest and best known member of this group and, as far as I can tell, was born outside of it. He would lead the “group” but by definition we have no leaders and cannot be led.

In many ways this is the story of North America and the United States as a whole. Our ancestors who settled this country, like Elon, left comfortable existences or escaped tragedy and came here with little idea of what they were going to do, how they were going to survive, or where they would end up. They were inherent risk takers and they built the civilization that eventually went to the Moon and beyond. Our early settlers, like Elon, knew that this was the place where opportunity existed and the best of all possible places to make dreams a reality. They were rogues in the truest sense of the term, and we are proud followers of this tradition.” - Jim Cantrell, Quora answer on Sept 2, 2015

“The Moon and Mars are often thought of as some escape hatch for rich people, but it won’t be that at all,” he said at music and tech conference South by Southwest *Sunday. «For the early people that go to Mars, it will be far more dangerous.*

“It kind of reads like Shackleton’s ad for arctic explorers: difficult, dangerous, good chance you’ll die, excitement for those who survive.

But for those who go, opportunity awaits. “There is going to be an explosion of entrepreneurial activity, because Mars will need everything from iron foundries to pizza joints,” Musk said.

For the billionaire himself, that vision of forging a new frontier as an explorer is part of a mindset that’s fueled his success: focusing on optimism and rejecting limitations. For early people who go to Mars, it will be far more dangerous.

“You want to wake up in the morning and think the future is going to be great, and that’s what being a spacefaring civilization is all about,” Musk said at the International Astronautical Congress in 2017. “It’s about believing in the future and thinking that the future will be better than the past. And I can’t think of anything more

exciting than going out there and being among the stars."

Life on Mars is a goal of Musk's SpaceX, which aims to use reusable rockets to eventually create "a self-sustaining civilization" there, according to the company's website. At South by Southwest in 2013, Musk said he would personally go to Mars when the company could continue running in his absence.

"I will go if I can be assured that SpaceX would go on without me," he said. "I've said I want to die on Mars, just not on impact."

Although Musk has a lot to say about the end of the world on Earth — predicting artificial intelligence and an impending World War 3 may destroy civilization — remaining focused on improvement is a key driver for him.

"There are a lot of negative things in the world. There are a lot of terrible things that are happening all over the world, all the time," said Musk during an appearance on a panel for HBO's show "Westworld" at South by Southwest. "There are lots of problems that need to get solved, there are lots of things that are miserable and kind of get you down."

But Musk advises finding purposeful work and focusing on the positive change you can affect.

"Life cannot just be about solving one miserable problem after another, that can't be the only thing," he says. "There need to be things that inspire you, that make you glad to wake up in the morning and be part of humanity."

For him, that's what makes tackling space flight, electric vehicles, tunnels, artificial intelligence, and perhaps a new media venture, worthwhile pursuits.

"The thing that drives me is that I want to be able to think about the future and feel good about that," Musk said in 2017 to the National Governors Association. "That we're doing what we can to have the future be as good as possible, to be inspired by what is likely to happen and to look forward to the next day.

"That's what really drives me, is trying to figure out how to make sure things are great." - Elon Musk explains his motivation to succeed: *"There need to be things that inspire you."* - by Ali Montag

Chapter 4 - Curiosity – The Necessary Root of Invention

Musk has an insatiable appetite for understanding the world around him. He speaks often of how much he read as a boy and a youth. His reading resulted in his being years ahead of his peers in his understanding of the rudiments of knowledge. But beyond that, his curiosity resulted in his digging deeply into hundreds of subjects, primarily in the fields of science, math, history, and philosophy.

All humans have natural curiosity, but from an early age the culture tends to discourage it with adages such as "curiosity killed the cat." It goes without saying that the more curious one is, the more likely they are to head for adventure, and adventure has potential for peril. So, some parents and many teachers discourage the most curious among us; whereas, wise parents and teachers would applaud curiosity at every chance.

You might find it curious, as I did, that psychologists are only recently delving into issues such as happiness, joy, forgiveness, gratitude, and *curiosity*. The first real looks at the underpinnings of curiosity started appearing in the 1950s, with another wave of interest in trying to measure curiosity in the 1980s. Only in the twenty-first century are we considering the usefulness of curiosity in producing a full life.

Einstein said it very well, "I have no special talents. I am only passionately curious." This is true of the typical entrepreneur and especially Elon Musk, the poster child for entrepreneurship.

Musk looks at the crazy traffic in West Los Angeles, but unlike the other millions of Los Angelenos stuck on the 405 freeway, he says: "What can we do about this?"

He does not think that going vertical with flying cars is a good idea because of the resulting noise pollution. He does not think that adding more rapid transit of the type now being employed is the answer because it requires too much surface area. So, he wonders about going underground. No, not like the regular subways, but using small tunnels and lots of them. And he imagines them going very, very deep so that heavy traffic can move without delays.

Then he imagines these tunnels containing 150 mph skates that could hold an individual car or a small 16 passenger buses. The mind of an entrepreneur operates by asking, "What if? How can we make something better?" Sometimes we just need to make it a different color, or size, or cost, or upside down. Or move it way, way underground. The entrepreneur then follows the trail of the idea as far as necessary to either learn the possibilities, contemplate solutions, and move towards action, or save the newly mined information for another day.

How Do We Become More Curious?

So, I was curious about this? I am naturally very, very curious. I loved the bookmobile and the library as a child and always checked out the maximum number of books. I am constantly surprised that others are not so curious. So, of course I googled: "How can I become more curious?"

If you want to be more curious, **you'll need to make the decision to do so**. That is step one in almost any process of change.

Then you'll need a "why." You see, making the decision will get you through the day, but by the next morning other priorities will take over. If you have a "why" that you actually care about deeply, you have a chance of actually achieving some real results. Your "why" might be a desire for self-improvement, a specific need to innovate in your field, or a hope that greater curiosity might lead to new adventure (Think Frodo.)

Next, you'll want to **learn to be an amazing listener and questioner**. This will be true in conversations with those who know about the subject, but also in passive reading, listening, or watching media regarding the subject you are curious about. You see, curiosity begets curiosity. Spend a few hours watching TED Talks. You should find yourself following up the TED talk with research into the subject matter that you found intriguing.

Listening – God gave us two ears and one mouth for a reason. Do you listen twice as much as you speak in most gatherings? When you speak, is it often to dig deeper into the life of those in your conversation group or to create more constructive analysis of the subject at hand? Or do you turn the subject to your own life, fail to validate the ideas of others, and take the conversation to the mundane or superficial?

Every conversation you have, whether analog or virtual, has the potential to further stimulate your curiosity, build upon your knowledge, and bring about potential solutions to issues you are considering. But it is very easy to quash the potential for meaningful talk.

Humans have an inborn interest in knowing and being known. This is the essence of intimacy. We have an outsized desire to be more intimate with others, but that desire is inhibited by our fear of being outed as foolish, wrong, or even just out of step. If I tell you my deepest thoughts, fears, hopes, and expectations, I have handed you a loaded weapon that you can use to destroy those very precious items I've placed in your care.

Owners and managers who can be *trusted* with the questions, ideas, and opinions of their downline will often find a wellspring of potential from folks they might never have given much consideration to in the past. Nourish those ideas with affirmation and encouragement. Both you and your employee will benefit.

Musk is notorious for factory briefings. While some feel that he is testing their knowledge, those in the know say that he is building on his own understanding.

Questioning – **question everything**! Do you believe that most men prefer the color blue? When someone says that to you or you read it in a book, you might just skip past it without giving it a thought. Or you might wonder what percent feel that way? What color is in second place? What colors do women prefer? Does color preference change with age? Do men in all cultures have the same preferences? Why do men prefer blue? How does this preference effect buying decisions, mating choices, productivity in the workplace?

Musk suggests that in looking at a problem or seeking a new direction, always go back to first principles. We will discuss this in detail later. But for now, the subject at hand is curiosity. You can't possibly contemplate the basic principles of a problem without a massive dose of curiosity.

As your mind reaches out along these various pathways of inquiry, you have the option to pursue or not pursue the answers based on your own personality, lens, and needs at the time. But the very act of questioning opens the mind and creates a habit. The person who is always questioning will meet a lot of resistance from peers who might feel threatened by your ideas. It will sometimes be hard when you feel as though you are the single voice offering a new direction against a chorus of "Why fix what ain't broken?" Exercising curiosity has its own sets of challenges, but most who decide to follow their curiosity will agree that the potential for great achievement is worth a little pain.

Musk would say that going against established approaches is what he does every day. In every case, he has to listen to a chorus of experts predicting that he will fail.

One thing that seems to be true of all the great tech giants, including Musk – they are all lifetime learners, and this means they are readers. Some report reading a book a day. Does that seem impossible or outlandish. What if you changed the way you are spending time on various screens watching cat videos, game shows, binging Netflix, and playing games, but used the time to read useful books, articles, and blogs? If you spend even an hour a day reading, you can't help but become curious about the content.

You will need to embrace the possibility of having your mind changed. Rigidity of stance is not helpful. Don't take any ideas or solutions off the table during the information gathering stage. Over time, if you are open, you will see potential for new directions. Discard reasoning like "that will never work," or "it's been tried before."

If you want to really raise the ire of Musk, just say that something he wants to do is impossible. This is a very fast way to get fired. Musk seems to take a perverse pleasure in personally proving that the very thing considered to be impossible can be done.

Communicate your new observations, ideas, and questions with others and in person with friends, associates, co-workers, suppliers, and customers. Debate, brainstorm, and challenge boundaries and old ways of thinking. Consider and don't trash crazy ideas. Some of the craziest notions turn into great companies. Elon Musk wants humans to have a backup plan on Mars. Now he owns a rocket company that launches more payloads than any sovereign country.

Finally, don't strain for new ideas. Let them come. Most great innovators have their best ideas and worst ideas just before falling asleep or just after waking when the mind is doing the work. Try asking a question, then blanking your mind from external thoughts, and drifting into a half sleep. You'll be amazed. Musk says his best ideas come in the shower.

Chapter 5 –
Observation - Seeing the
Forest and the Trees

For some odd reason, I can recall the first time I heard the saying about not seeing the forest for the trees. I remember that the idea made no sense to me. Now I've come to believe that the opposite can be true as well. Some folks can't see the trees for the forest.

The really great entrepreneurs are good at seeing the big picture without losing site of the details. To do this requires observation. The kind of observation we will talk about is about using our senses and then interpreting what our senses are observing.

I have been accused of being an absent-minded professor, having my head continually in the clouds, and but for the fact that my head is securely attached to my neck, a likely candidate for leaving my head on the car rooftop while driving away. Many creatives have these same characteristics. This is fantastic for invention, vision, big picture thinking, and the like. It is not good for making sure the product name is spelled correctly on the package.

Alternatively, there were thousands of rocket scientists over the past 60+ years who were so focused on the details of getting payloads into space safely that they never took a longer look at the potential opportunities for radically changing everything about the industry through lowering costs.

Musk wanted to colonize Mars. Given current approaches, the cost would be astronomical. Much like one who appreciates impressionistic art, he had to back up halfway across the room, and take the longer look at the business of rockets.

He observed that the greatest expense of the rocket is largely made up of construction materials. He asked the question, "Can the cost of those materials be substantially reduced?"

He then observed that unlike cars or trucks or airplanes, rockets got used once and then thrown away. The Space Shuttles were reusable, but very expensive to construct. He asked the question, "Couldn't we find a way to reuse the boosters on rockets which represent 70% of the cost?" Then later, "Couldn't we reuse the rocket and the fairings?"

With the successful butt-down landings of the booster, Musk was able to dramatically lower the cost per mission. Near misses with the fairings would seem to offer substantial hope that they, too, will be reused in the not too distant future.

A single observation – cost per launch can be lowered – has created a complete disruption of the rocket industry and created huge potential for benefits not even under consideration until two years ago.

Trees and Branches Approach

Musk believes that when you are studying a subject, you need to understand the core principles first. This might be akin to UCLA basketball Coach John Wooden's famous quote about fundamentals when he addressed the top high school recruits in the US at their first practice under his leadership: "This, gentlemen, is a basketball."

> Musk says: *"It is important to view knowledge as sort of a semantic tree. Make sure you understand the fundamental principles, ie the trunk and big branches, before you get into the leaves/details or there is nothing for them to hang on to."*

If you are going to get into the urban transportation business, where would you start? You might begin with the history of land transportation, including the most recent history of things like urban train systems, double decker freeways, HOV lanes, onramp light systems, electronic sensors in the surface of the freeways, cameras monitoring the freeways, and apps designed to navigate the fastest way to any destination. You might want to look at other similar systems such as other flow systems (e.g. water or air) or current cost/benefit analysis of various transportation systems, etc.

These together might be a way of constructing the trunk of the tree. Any one of those might create a potential branch worthy of more study. How effective is the data accumulation through embedded electrical contacts, cameras, and GPS from smart phones in cars? What kinds of things can we learn from flow analysis of liquids in various systems that might result in better flow for cars? What are the various materials being used for roadbeds, and why?

After a thorough analysis of the trunk items, the even more detailed analysis of the branches that seem to offer the most potential for solutions, questions begin to arise. Could cars have data collection devices added to them that would benefit throughput of cars during rush hour? What data is not being collected that would create an opportunity to move cars more efficiently? What materials are being overlooked that might be substantially cheaper or less labor intensive for road beds? Why are trucks and cars intermingled on the same freeways? Should lane changes be more restricted than they are? Do HOV lanes actually do anything to help?

What About the Details?

O.K. so we don't want to fail to see the forest, but what about having the forest obscure our view of the trees? Could anything be more obvious than the critical importance of observing the details of sending rockets into space? Once we have observed the basics and reached some conclusions about how to proceed, the great entrepreneurs are mindful of even the most minor details.

Just today as I write this (December 24, 2018), Musk has tweeted that the new version of the BFR, now called Starship, will use specialized stainless steel instead of carbon fiber:

> "Yup. Actually, the only significant design element in common with early Atlas is stainless steel & we're using a different alloy mix. I super ♥ 300 Series Stainless!"

With what we know right this minute, we can't know if Musk was intimately involved with the decision to use this alloy. However, we do know about his detail orientation.

We do know that during the ramp up of Tesla 3, Musk was sleeping at the factory. We know that he invited any and every worker at the factory to bring him issues and ideas for improvement. We do know that he goes where the problem is and participates fully in the approaches to fixing the issues that pop up. We know that he answers consumers directly regarding their issues with any Tesla product.

> We also know that *"He would trap an engineer in the SpaceX factory and set to work grilling him about a type of valve or specialized material. I thought at first that he was challenging me to see if I knew my stuff,"* said Kevin Brogan, one of the early engineers. *"Then I realized he was trying to learn things. He would quiz you until he learned ninety percent of what you know."* - <u>Elon Musk: Tesla, SpaceX, and the Quest for a Fantastic Future</u>

Musk has also reported that during the design stages of each automobile, a weekly meeting takes place to go "over every inch of the design." He participates in this meeting because he literally intends to "go over every inch." And not just once, but with different lighting and from every angle, so that the car looks beautiful and functions perfectly in every condition.

What does it take to get better at the details? To begin with, it takes focus. The very definition of focus implies that we want details. However, most of us spend most of our day with little or no focus on ideas, tasks, or solutions. In fact, because of our devices, we may be the least focused humans in history. Even as I type this manuscript, my computer is sending me notifications about emails, Skypes, and news, begging me to notice them instead of focusing on the work. My smart phone is nine inches away, enticing me to check the stock market, the weather or send out a text.

Musk offers a solution. He breaks his day into 5-minute chunks. During this time-limited period, he works on just a single subject, and allows no distractions. In this way he has almost no choice but to give intent focus to the issue at hand for that chunk of time.

We sometimes use this method in our MasterMind groups. (My partner, Craig Korotko, and I currently facilitate five mastermind groups where business people come together to help one another grow personally and professionally.) We give each member about 5 minutes to posit one issue that is on their mind, and the remaining time is for the group to respond. It is amazing to see how much brainstorming can take place within that 5 minutes.

I have no access to Musk's calendar to see what has made his to do list on any given day, but I imagine it to be something like this:

7:00 – 7:05 – What can be done about fit and finish complaints on Model 3
7:05 – 7:10 – Find a way to speed up battery line at station 5. Seems to be a bottleneck there
7:10 – 7:15 – Gigafactory in China is behind schedule two days – create strategy for getting back on track
7:15 – 7:20 – Received call asking for quote on water tunnel. Do we want to distract from transportation options at this time?

And so, it would go. Now, creating such a list for an eight-hour day would take about an hour. However, the very exercise of creating the list focuses the mind on the most critical issues and sets in motion the creative process.

As mentioned, Musk states that his best ideas come during his morning shower. He believes that the relaxing moments after waking are times when the brain's effort during sleep finds purchase.

You may think that 5-minute chunks are not going to work for you. Make them 10-minutes or even longer. It might be useful to take a minute right now and start writing down a schedule for tomorrow. It will seem that you are just creating a list, but instead of a list that you sort through during the day, picking off the easy ones first, this is a schedule to follow. Musk also recommends listing the tasks in order of highest value. Others recommend ordering these items by difficulty. Yet others suggest chunking your entire day based on your body rhythms.

Chapter 6 –
Expertise in Every Aspect
of the Business

Many who hear this admonition are seriously ready to stop reading. The curiosity part seemed fun, and some of you are already blessed (or cursed) with a huge amount of that asset. On the other hand, becoming an expert sounds like something that could take massive amounts of time and hard work. It might even entail spending money on books, tutors, college classes, or consultants.

It really depends on the subject matter. With Google at your fingertips, you can become a world class expert in many subjects, quickly and effortlessly. At one point in my life, I badly needed to become an expert in how plastic caps thread onto water bottles to make a seal that doesn't leak. There are many, many articles on the topic on the internet. My suppliers provided more ideas. My team brainstormed. Within about ten hours, I probably knew more about creating a leakproof water bottle than anyone in any group of 1 million people. You see, almost no one wants to become an expert regarding water bottles that won't leak. This would also be true of Giant Swallowtails or the small wineries of Napa, other subjects on which I could lay claim to being an expert. What should you become an expert at?

Elon Musk tried to find rocket scientists that could help him make less expensive rockets. He didn't find what he needed, so if he wanted to achieve his goal, he needed to become a rocket scientist. This takes a little longer and requires quite a bit of math, physics, chemistry, and more. I don't want to become a rocket scientist, nor do I think I have the chops to study and become one. Musk did. He read, studied, met with experts, listened, asked questions, and became an expert. He is now arguably the best rocket scientist ever, doing things with rockets that no one has ever done before.

Musk is no different than many who are reading this book. He is faced with the same trials and difficulties. The difference is that he asks the question, "how hard could it be?

> *"I never had a job where I made anything physical. I cofounded two Internet software companies, Zip2 and PayPal. So, it took me a few years to kind of learn rocket science, if you will.*
>
> *I had to learn how you make hardware. I'd never seen a CNC machine or laid out carbon fibre. I didn't know any of these things. But if you read books and talk to experts, you'll pick it up pretty quickly. [...] It's really pretty straightforward. Just read books and talk to people–particularly books. The data rate of reading is much greater than when somebody's talking. "You can learn whatever you need to do to start a successful business either in school or out of school. A school, in theory, should help accelerate that process, and I think oftentimes it does. It can be an efficient learning process, perhaps more efficient than empirically learning lessons. There are examples of successful entrepreneurs who never graduated high school, and there are those that have PhD's. I think the important principle is to be dedicated to learning what you need to know, whether that is in school or empirically."*

The Boring Company

Instead of complaining about LA traffic, he set out to change it. Transportation is obviously within his area of expertise, but building tunnels wasn't. If you started right now, you could research the methods for building tunnels and in a very short time, you'd know more than almost anyone alive. Musk did just that. As a result of his research, he came to believe that tunnel building was extremely inefficient, and that if efficiencies could be improved, it might be possible to take all urban roadways underground.

Musk, almost on a whim, created The Boring Company. In just two years Musk took the idea from inception to a test tunnel in Hawthorne, California. Company officials report that they are inundated with requests to invest in the company, and that proposals for other types of tunnels (utilities, water) are also coming in from governments and companies around the world.

But how does this apply to you and me, mere mortals? Years ago, I was involved in a transportation issue in Los Angeles that caused me to need to become an expert on carpool lanes. While wading through mountains of materials on freeway transportation, I developed an idea about how to build an automated, elevated pod system that is not that different from Musk's approach by tunnel. The huge difference is that the tunnel method allows for layers and layers of duplication without unsightly, noisy infrastructure. Musk's plan also provides for cars, freight, buses, bikes, and pedestrians to all use the same throughways.

The point that we don't want to lose sight of is that everyone of us is capable of becoming the expert and then applying that expertise to issues around us.

Maybe you want to build a business around something simpler, like baking pies. If you really applied yourself, you could become an expert in the informational aspect of baking pies in about 40-60 hours. You'd start with the basics regarding history, materials, baking methods, fills, etc. Some of that research might cause you to think about different kinds of ovens and their benefits, baking times and heats, or the chemistry of the dough. In each case, you'd be constantly asking yourself "what if" questions and considering out-of-the-box solutions. Then, you might use another 60 hours to do the baking and testing the results.

You would potentially hire a pie chef for 20 hours of training. You'd test the best recipes. You'd read, listen to podcasts, and watch YouTube videos, relentlessly. Your curiosity would cause you to ask questions that don't fit current thinking. Would a radish work well in a pie? How about Butterfingers? What if you deep fried a pie? Would Vermont's best maple syrup be good over apple pie? What if you made them deeper, used more crust, used less crust, made an open-face pie or upside-down pie?

Maybe less than one in one-million have done this much work on pies. At the end of your effort, you would undoubtedly be an expert. You might even be in the top 10% of all pie experts. And you might have some interesting ways to differentiate yourself from the competition.

Why would you want to become an expert? Let me count the ways:

1. Become credible in the eyes of potential clients
2. Improve decision making on any subject
3. Invent new solutions to problems
4. Create a new business around your expertise
5. Improve processes in your existing business
6. Get paid to write articles in print or online
7. Teach others for fun or profit
8. Know how to help others

Without thinking much about it you've probably already done a lot of this in your life. Here are just a few of the areas where I've applied the methods suggested here.

- Became a nationally recognized expert in padlocks (publications, paid teaching)
- Became the top national expert in bicycle flat prevention (manufactured solution)
- Became an expert in how to blog for lawyers (paid to do so)
- Became an expert in how to optimize Google My Business (blogs, videos)
- Became an expert in Teen Sexual Purity (appeared on Geraldo Daytime Show in 1995)
- Became top national expert in Bicycle Retailing (5 published books)
- Became a recognized expert in how to run a small business (Published by Inc., Warner)
- Became an expert in how to become an expert

The list could be ten times that long, but you are probably already bored to tears over my exploits. So, let's cut to the chase. The methods below will help you to become a serious expert compared to the vast majority of people, and even compared to the vast majority of those in the field you are interested in pursuing. Because you gain substantial expertise in a short period of time doesn't mean that you will always want to stop there. You can obviously pile on your credibility by continuing to research and by doing your own studies and analysis.

For instance, my appearance on Geraldo would not have happened after using my three-hour method. However, I could have written great blog posts within 3 hours, done guest blogs, and started ramping up to print articles or do radio interviews with not much more than 3 hours of work.

One last caveat. This process doesn't apply to an entire profession. You can't become an expert on the law in 3 hours. You can, however become an expert in less than 3 hours on the laws associated with texting and driving.

Step 1. Select the Area of Expertise Carefully

Take five minutes or maybe ten to plan. This may be something you skip if you want to become an instant expert on the tiny red bumps on your toddler's back. But in most cases, you will want to think about what you want to accomplish by gaining the expertise, and what the specific expertise required might look like.

Let's say that you want to become an expert in dog breeding. My son bought a golden retriever and thought he might get rich breeding him. The analysis started with these questions: would I want to become an expert in dogs? Golden retrievers? Breeding methods for dogs? Of course, I wanted to know how to make money breeding golden retrievers. That took me less than one hour to become a credible expert with enough knowledge to write an article suitable for publication.

Word to the wise: "Suitable for publication" doesn't always mean suitable for making an investment. I would have wanted to spend at least another 20 hours researching the breeding of golden retrievers before actually going forward.

Step 2. Google the Expertise Exactly

In this case, you'd want to Google exactly as stated and using the terms: How to Make Money Breeding Golden Retrievers. You will find almost 6 million results on that subject. But you don't have time to read 6,000,000 responses.

So quickly read through the summaries of the articles offered and make a decision about where to start. You might go to several websites before you find one that is going to be your gold mine.

Step 3. Go Deep!!

Most net surfers and researchers are very impatient. They won't even scroll down on page one for more ideas. Only 20% will go to page two in the search results. If you want to find the folks who know what they are talking about, you may have to scroll down 10 or 20 pages. You see, Google does their best to provide you with the most relevant content first, but they don't always successfully prioritize. Moreover, some internet-savvy folks are able to get under-researched content highly ranked, and some serious content providers know nothing about search engine optimization and end up with that content really far down in rank.

Change up your search if it isn't working. Use different search terms such as "breeding tips for golden retrievers." You could go really broad and use "dog breeding tips," or how to breed my dog."

Also follow "good" rabbit trails. When you are on some websites, the content may not be helpful, but the links might be even better. The deeper you go into the subject, the more likely you are to find the great site, and you may also start refining your subject and, therefore, your search results.

Step 4. YouTube and Other Resources

As a researcher, I love YouTube. There is a reason YouTube is the 2nd most used search engine. By using all the same techniques as above for Google Search, you can uncover some fabulous videos on your subject. But not just on YouTube. You might also want to check out:

- Amazon.com - Find a book on the subject. Maybe it is on Kindle. Or you may need to wait a few days to get it. Either way, a great book can help deepen your knowledge.
- Library - How old school. Encyclopedias, other resources not online, books no longer selling on Amazon. The bigger the library the better. (https://www.worldcat.org – the world's largest library)
- Images - Put your best keywords into Google and view the images. Sometimes that will lead to a great and informative website. (e.g. which red bumps look like the red bumps on your toddler's back).
- industry sites - Is there an association, a magazine, or other resources that may or may not have online content? For many research topics this will be the case. You may need to go to the association website or a magazine's website to find PDF's or old issues.
- Trade shows – You can commonly learn more in a few hours of walking a trade show than you will with a Google Search.
- Follow blogs, YouTube Channels, podcasts or other expert resources. Establish relationships with these experts by making comments. Then reach out through email, Linkedin, or Twitter to establish a personal bond.

Step 5. Start Telling Others What You Know

Almost every interview with Musk includes many references to his partners, collaborators, team members, and even friends. He says that he has two resources for feedback, books (by which we can assume he means all aspects of research available today) and talking about things with others.

Nothing beats teaching as a method of solidifying knowledge and finding out what you're missing that might be critical. Tell your spouse, your best friend, your mom or anyone else who will listen about the cool new stuff you've learned. Write about it in your blog if appropriate. Writing it out will also stimulate you to consider what additional information might be needed or might increase the interest level of the story. Writing clarifies what you know and what you don't know.

For most subjects, you should have been able to complete the online research portion in three hours or less. Is it enough for what you need? In most cases, probably. But if you want to become one of the top experts on the very narrow topic that you've chosen, you can then take it to the next level.

Business Expertise

If you are going to own or be the CEO of a business, you need broader expertise in such things as accounting, finance, marketing, sales, processes, human resources, and the product and services you offer. In my experience most small business owners are far from being experts in these critical skills.

Chapter 7
Analysis Is an Acquired Skill

When brainstorming is done correctly, there is a critically important rule that determines the success of the brainstorming effort: ***there are no bad ideas***. The theory is that you want everyone to feel that they can be completely free to suggest whatever pops into their mind. Sometimes, however, we see suggestions that beg to be ridiculed. But here's an amazing big take away. Sometimes those very bad ideas turn out to be the germ of a huge winner after more brainstorming and ***analysis.***

When you've become an expert and you are super curious and you allow your brain to do the work, you are going to have ideas. It bears repeating with a twist that Musk says most of his great ideas have come in the shower, just before dozing off, or at Burning Man. He states that he believes that this is the result of the mind doing the work during rest, and then the ideas often come during down times. Where do your most creative ideas occur?

An idea might appear to be so amazing that you wonder why no one has ever thought of it before. You begin to envision factories churning out your new product and you piling up your first fortune.

Sometimes after a bit of analysis, it turns out there's a good reason why no one has ever made that product or offered that service before. And you certainly want to know that before you bet the family 401k on your clever idea.

At other times, the issue isn't whether the idea is good or bad, but whether it is feasible given your finances, time, competitive restraints, and more.

I had an amazing idea about seven years ago. I believed that a Bluetooth finger ring (with a haptic alert) associated with your iPhone would sell like crazy. I was always forgetting to turn on my phone after church and off in various meetings. Or, I would leave the phone downstairs and not hear the ringer. A ring with a haptic to signal me would mean I'd just leave the audible ringer on the phone off at all times.

I still think it would have sold great. But I would have needed to go way outside my comfort zone and try to find someone in China that I could trust to develop this electronic device. I had blown a large sum just a year before on an amazing idea for an app, but the offshore app company couldn't quite get it to work. So, I hesitated to move forward.

After considering how much time I'd have to take, the total cost of getting it made and to market, and the lost opportunity cost of my time in other ventures, I passed on the ring idea, so it is now an open source idea, and you can make it if you like. My analysis caused me to pass. If I'd been 20-years younger, had more financial resources, and less on my plate, it might have been a go.

Elon Musk has famously said that entering the auto business was foolish, especially with an electric car, and especially since he would be competing with some of the biggest companies in the world. He also said that it was foolish to build rockets in competition with Boeing and the largest countries on earth. All of his friends told him not to do either, but he analyzed the situation and figured it was worth the try. For him, with the fortune he had already amassed from the sale of PayPal, he could afford to risk the money and the time.

Humans are constantly analyzing. When we feel sick, we analyze the symptoms to determine the possible methods for relief or cure. Each month most of us analyze the way we will stretch the few dollars in our account until the next check. After each football play, we analyze the performance of the team, the coaches, the players, and sometimes even the refs. Analysis is necessary to daily living, but not all of us are great at analyzing situations. Those who are best at analysis do these things:

- Start by looking at first principles
- Do lots of research

- Ask great questions
- Break down the analysis into categories
- Isolate the strengths and weaknesses
- Quickly determine what needs more research
- Find additional human resources as necessary
- Seek out and listen to negative feedback
- Make hard decisions quickly

Step 1. Start by Looking at First Principles

BARRY HURD: How do you train yourself to think differently and surround yourself with people that do that as well? Or maybe you don't do that. I mean, how do you get into an organization?

ELON MUSK: I think, generally, their {other people's} thinking process is too bound by convention or analogy to prior experiences. So it's very rare that people try to think of something on a first principles basis. They'll say, "We'll do that because it's always been done that way." Or they'll not do it because, "Well, nobody has ever done that. So it must not be good." But that's just a ridiculous way to think.

I mean, you have to build up the reasoning from the ground up from first principles as in the phrase that's used in physics. So, you look at the fundamentals and construct your reasoning from that and then see if you have a conclusion that works or doesn't work. And it may or may not be different from what people have done in the past. It's harder to think that way, though. Sorry.

BARRY HURD: Why is it so hard to think that way? And how have you managed to? I mean, obviously, you've thought the other way. How have you broken that path?

ELON MUSK: I don't know. I've just always thought that way, I suppose. I mean, I would always think about something and whether that thing was really true or not. Could something else be true or is there a better conclusion that one could draw that's more probable? I don't know. I was doing that when I was in elementary school. And I would just question things. Or, maybe, it's sort of built-in [to our nature] to question things. The Henry Ford – Interview

https://www.thehenryford.org/explore/stories-of-innovation/
visionaries/elon-musk/

Somebody could say, "Battery packs are really expensive and that's just the way they will always be... Historically, it has cost $600 per kilowatt hour. It's not going to be much better than that in the future."

With first principles, you say, "What are the material constituents of the batteries? What is the stock market value of the material constituents?"

It's got cobalt, nickel, aluminum, carbon, some polymers for separation and a seal can. Break that down on a material basis and say, "If we bought that on the London Metal Exchange what would each of those things cost?"

It's like $80 per kilowatt hour. So clearly you just need to think of clever ways to take those materials and combine them into the shape of a battery cell and you can have batteries that are much, much cheaper than anyone realizes." Interview with Kevin Rose

Most innovation or invention comes from incremental changes to an existing approach or by changing something to be more like something that has been done or another product, called reasoning by analogy: make smart phones larger, smaller, different colors, add more lenses to the camera feature, take away a port to make room for more battery. These types of incremental changes should not be dismissed as meaningless or second class, and obviously Musk and every other innovator uses this approach:

As *CleanTechnica* reports

"Everything at Tesla undergoes a continual process of analysis and incremental improvement, and the Gigafactory assembly lines are no exception. Jerome Guillen told CNBC that the company is working to improve the yield, throughput, and capacity of each production line. Again, this not only increases the number of cells produced but also improves the company's financial picture. Making more batteries from the same line translates to a better return on the capital invested in each line."

Since reasoning and innovating are an important part of all creative work, Musk is constantly encouraging his staff to go back to first principles.

How do you ascertain the first principles in any situation? You question every assumption about the product or service. Let's try a very simple example that was not from the Elon Musk list.

I observed that the use of a peer-to-peer approach in business problem solving was helping small business owners to achieve great success in a short time. Since helping small business owners in this way is a prime personal goal for my life, I immediately began questioning the best method for creating and sustaining such groups, including the mastermind approach.

There were plenty of examples of mastermind approaches online, so I did the research. The first principles turned out to be:

- What is the optimum group size?
- How often should a group meet?
- How long should a meeting last?
- How much should a membership cost?
- How should the meeting be structured?
- How do you maximize retention of members?
- How do you find members?

Each of those questions then needed subordinate questions, research and answers. But by determining first principles, the newly formed business was not a copy of any other mastermind group but had some approaches that were new. Not everything was new, of course. Some were copied and some were incremental changes to existing groups.

You can use this approach on any business idea, new product, new service, or even new internal methodology such as bookkeeping or prospecting for new customers. Musk has done this in a major way by seeing his factories as products:

"We realized that the true problem, the true difficulty, and where the greatest potential is – is building the machine that makes the machine. In other words, it's building the factory. I'm really thinking of the factory like a product."

Referring to the Gigafactory: *"[We] plan to package the battery plant into a product to be able to reproduce it."*

Speaking about the solar cell production at the Gigafactory, Musk has pointed out that in looking to first principles it became apparent that he should not manufacture the panels. They were a commodity. The potential for cost reduction was in the balance of the product, so Tesla makes everything else.

What about your company? Consider every part of what you make or do? Break it down into first principles, then mercilessly innovate with breakthrough ideas, create completely different approaches, and then incrementally improve the resulting product, service, or process.

Step 2 - Do lots of research

We have already covered the research aspect a few times above. However, allow me to take this idea one step further. There is no way to put a value on the benefits of good counsel. The Internet is a fabulous resource for research, but it is also fatally limited in that it is only reporting, not actually doing the work of science, engineering, and even tinkering.

Thomas Edison was the Elon Musk of his time. His inventions are still lighting our way and bring fabulous sights and sounds into our homes and cars. But Edison was part scientist, part engineer, and by all means a tinkerer. It is said that he tried 1000 different approaches to the lightbulb before he found one that worked. Was each iteration based on science and engineering? Not at all. Many were just the result of the "try this to see if it works" technique.

Mistakes during research and tinkering often result in breakthroughs. New ideas beget ideas that would likely have never been considered but for the first idea being experimented upon. As noted earlier, ideas that seem far-fetched or even dumb are often the springboard for an idea that changes everything.

Does your company do research? Do you have brainstorming sessions? Do you invite all levels of employees to help brainstorm ideas? Do you reward innovation? Are you known as an employer who is open to change? Are you known in your field as an innovator?

Plenty of companies do just fine by copying the best. I'm just assuming that you are reading this book because you want to be a bit more "Muskian." Musk spends his own personal time and plenty of his money and energy on research.

Step 3 - Ask great questions

Throughout the process of analyzing any product, service, or process, the solutions are commonly arrived at because the right question was asked.

> Elon Musk - *"[The Hitchhikers Guide to the Galaxy] taught me that* **the tough thing is figuring out what questions to ask, but that once you do that, the rest is really easy.** *I came to the conclusion that we should aspire to increase the scope and scale of human consciousness in order to better understand what questions to ask."*

What in the world are the right questions? You might start with the journalists' list: Who, What, When, Where, and How? Then add a huge one, Why, and then Why Not?

The key is to question everything:

> *"I would rather have questions that can't be answered than answers that can't be questioned."* - Richard P. Feynman

> *"Then do not stop to think about the reasons for what you are doing, about why you are questioning. The important thing is not to stop questioning. Curiosity has its own reason for existence."* - Alfred Einstein

> *"If I had an hour to solve a problem and my life depended on the solution, I would spend the first 55 minutes determining the proper question to ask... for once I know the proper question, I could solve the problem in less than five minutes."* – Einstein

This last quotation from Einstein's really says it all, and so well that I almost hesitate to try to build upon it. But let's try a fun example. In one of my books, <u>When Friday Isn't Payday: How to Plan Start Build and Manage Your Small Business</u>, the questions that formed the basis for an entire book were:

Why are small business owners commonly unable to earn above $70,000 in personal income?

- Why are small business owners seemingly satisfied with less than $100,000 in income?
- What are some of the key, specific factors that would help owners create more income?
- What are some of the personality traits that might hold owners back from achieving more income?
- What are the skill traits that are holding them back?
- What are the habits that are holding them back?
- What the misconceptions that are holding them back?
- Who is the likely reader?
- What can I say that might help them achieve more income?
- What have others said that I can use?
- What teaching method is most likely to achieve results?
- What material has already appeared in other books?
- What is the competition in this space?
- How long should the book be so that it is not intimidating but credible?
- What title will entice readers to purchase it?
- What other titles on this topic have been successful?
- What other titles have failed?

The list was much longer than this, but can you see how the questions began to shape the book?

No matter how simple the issue, the questions you ask will be key to the success of the final decision, product, or process.

One amazingly successful approach to brainstorming is to ask the individuals who will be in the brainstorming session to produce a set of questions prior to the meeting. You can sort through the questions to determine those that make the most sense to you for organizing the brainstorming session.

Step 4 - Break down the analysis into categories

If you want to send a rocket to Mars for the purpose of colonizing the red planet, it is very likely that the issues involved will be more than you can wrap your mind around, even if you are Elon Musk. Just imagine for a moment, the complexity of such an undertaking. Add to the complexity, that you will have to invent many of the specific characteristics of the eventual solution, because current technology will not allow you to get there, much less with a massive payload, and return safely!

But even much simpler tasks are more than most humans can grasp. It may seem obvious to say that we must break down the analysis into categories, but we commonly rush headlong into a project based on assumptions rather than analysis.

I would like to buy glass doors for the library in my home. I could run over to Home Depot, look through the offerings, and buy the one I like the best. However, if I want optimal results, I will need to collect and analyze information, such as:

1. The look of the door
   a. Style
   b. Color
   c. Material
   d. Window finish
2. The cost of the door
3. The installation of the door
   a. Do it myself
   b. Hire someone
4. Where to find
   a. Quality
   b. Price
   c. Delivery
   d. Terms

My dad always said to measure twice and cut once. Asking the right questions, followed by creating categories for analysis is the measuring tool.

Step 5 - Isolate the strengths and weaknesses

In the lock business, we used to say that if you'll tell me what tool the thief is going to bring to the scene, I'll produce the lock that will stop him. Or put another way, I can build a vehicle that will protect everyone in that vehicle from death in any accident.

Every final solution is the result of compromises. Tanks, the solution to the vehicle suggested above, are too expensive and ugly to compete with cars. People are willing to take some risk of death in order to get the convenience and style of cars. In fact, some are willing to ride motorcycles.

Therefore, the next step in the innovation process is to examine the strengths and weaknesses of the proposition. Small business coaches use a method called SWOT, to examine the business as a whole, and/or products and services that are being offered by the business. SWOT stands for Strengths, Weaknesses, Opportunities, and Threats. If you would like, you can see a 31 page SWOT analysis for Tesla here.

The SWOT for your company might not require 31 pages, but most small companies have never done a SWOT for their company or for any of their products or services. By merely making a list of these for you company, you will undoubtedly gain great insight into potential ways for you to improve your company, products, services, and processes.

Step 6 - Determine what needs more research

Potentially, this step is too obvious by half. Unfortunately, many will rush pass this critical point. Clearly it is important to put more research into the weaknesses and the threats. It will be cheaper to find approaches that eliminate weaknesses and reduce threats prior to introducing the product or service.

However, it may be the greatest strength that offers the most return on investment for more research. It seems pretty likely that many, if not most of the prospects for the Tesla roadster, want a car that offers amazing performance. The lessons learned from the roadster that provided amazing acceleration and handling are now informing the other Tesla models; so much so that Musk's 4-door sedans are winning drag races against all comers.

But Musk doesn't stop with those victories. The new roadster is expected to be the best car ever in the ¼ mile and 0-60 mph categories. It takes a ton of research to top yourself in a category where you are already the acknowledged leader.

To paraphrase Musk...You never stop asking yourself questions.

Step 7 - Find additional human resources as necessary

When Musk decided that his $190 million would be enough to give him a real chance at some kind of effort to create excitement about space and ultimately expand man's reach to other habitable planets, he knew almost nothing about rocketry. He had shot off a few rockets in the backyard as a kid, and he knew more than the average citizen about physics, chemistry, and other important elements for getting into space, but he was certainly not a rocket scientist.

He began to research both the science and the people who could help him reach his lofty goals. One such important addition to the early team was Jim Cantrell. Jim was a very serious rocket engineer with huge amounts of experience in the space industry, both in the US and Russia.

Jim describes the process this way in a Quora answer:

> *He literally sucks the knowledge and experience out of people that he is around. He borrowed all of my college texts on rocket propulsion when we first started working together in 2001. We also hired as many of my colleagues in the rocket and spacecraft business that were willing to consult with him. It was like a gigantic spaceapalooza.* - June 7, 2016

Over and over you see Musk joining clubs, groups, interrogating employees and visiting companies who have the information he needs to keep asking the right questions, find optional solutions, and reach for more first principles.

Where do you find these resources? Check out that last paragraph again, and let me add to the list:

- Universities – clubs, professors, grad students
- Chambers of commerce – local, regional, national

- Clubs of all kinds – hobby clubs, service clubs, business organizations
- Supplier employees
- Your own employees
- Hire the specific expertise
- Contact a non-competitive company owner in your same basic business
- Industry associations
- Government commissions – local, regional, state, federal, international

Successful people use these techniques. Musk is known for asking prospective employees to tell him about problems they've overcome in the past, and the pathway they took to get to the solution. I once had a problem with a plastic part. I interviewed engineers with a single question: Here's the problem I have with this part. How would you go about solving the problem?

There are always plenty of human resources available to get to the answers you need. It is only a matter of thinking through the best way to find those resources.

Step 8 - Seek out and listen to negative feedback

Musk talks about an important part of his method for analyzing progress on any project. He calls it a feedback loop, which seeks to answer the question, "What is wrong with the product, service, process, or idea?" He says that he has almost no interest in hearing what a friend or customer likes about their Tesla. He wants to know what they thought needed attention or could have been done better.

Musk was asked to give advice to entrepreneurs during an interview with Kevin Rose:

"…so, I think in terms of advice I think it's very important to seek out, to actively seek out and listen very carefully to negative feedback. And this is something that people tend to avoid, because it's painful, but I think this is a very common mistake to not actively seek out and listen to negative feedback."

Most of us don't want to be a negative Nellie. If we are asked our opinion about a product or service, we are more inclined to give an honest, positive evaluation, concentrating on the things we like, or we give faint praise. This tendency is even more pronounced if we have a relationship with the "creator" of that which we are being called upon to judge.

Moreover, most creatives are not all that willing to hear the negative. When someone is honest, there is a huge tendency to defend against, dismiss, or deflect the criticism and move away from the critic.

This type of behavior is of little value to the enterprise, though it may temporarily protect the ego of the creator.

Instead, Musk would suggest you specifically challenge observers of your new idea to find the flaws, point out the negatives, and be honest about the overall idea.

> *On more than one occasion, Musk has asserted that this is his number one piece of advice for budding entrepreneurs.*

Step 9 - Do the Math

As I read through Ashlee Vance's fascinating Musk biography, I was taken with how often those around Musk were impressed with Musk's ability to do the math. When the Russians turned Musk down in his effort to acquire two ICBM's, his early SpaceX team were shocked when Musk developed a spread sheet showing that they could build their own rocket.

> *Musk had come to Russia filled with optimism about putting on a great show for mankind and was now leaving exasperated and disappointed by human nature. The Russians were the only ones with rockets that could possibly fit within Musk's budget. "It was a Long drive," Cantral said. "We sat there in silence looking at the Russian peasants shopping in the snow." The somber mood lingered all the way to the plane until the drink cart arrived. "You always feel particularly good when the wheels lift off in Mosco, Cantrell said. "It's like 'oh my God I made it.'" So Griffin and I got drinks and clicked our glasses. Musk sat in a row in front of them typing on a computer. We're thinking, "What can he be doing now?" At which*

point Musk wheeled around and flashed the spreadsheet he'd created. "Hey guys," he said. "I think we can build this rocket ourselves."

Griffin and Cantrell had downed a couple of drinks by this time and were too deflated to entertain a fantasy. They knew all too well the stories of gung-ho millionaires who thought they could conquer space only to lose their fortunes. Just the Year before, Andrew Bill, a real estate and finance whiz in Texas, folded his aerospace company after having poured millions into a massive test site. "We're thinking, 'yeah, you and whose army,'" Cantrell said. "But Elon says, "No, I'm serious. I have the spreadsheet. Musk passed his laptop over to Griffin and Cantrell, and they were dumbfounded. The document detailed the cost of the materials needed to build, assemble, and launch a rocket. According to his calculations he could undercut existing large companies by building a modest- sized rocket that would cater to a part of the market that specialized in carrying smaller satellites and research payloads into space. The spreadsheet also laid out the hypothetical performance characteristics of the rocket in fairly impressive detail." I said, 'Elon, where did you get this?'" Cantrell said. **Elon Musk: Tesla, SpaceX and the Quest for a Fantastic Future**

Elon Musk knows the math. He had created the spreadsheet. In truth, there may be nothing other than his grit that is more important to the survival of his enterprises. It can't be said often enough, "You can't manage what you don't count."

Over and over again I have met with company CEO's who have no idea what their margins are or should be for that type of business. Many don't even know their break-even point. Others can't even give an estimate about where sales are for the week, the month-to-date, or how this year's sales compare to last year's.

When in negotiations with company owners, they are often unable to quickly evaluate their options in order to make the best deal possible, and as a result they leave money on the table or lose a profitable deal altogether.

Know your costs. Know your margins. Know what your overhead contribution is. One retailer I know met with me and was quite happy.

He had just completed a $10,000 sale and made a cool $2000. In most retail situations, a 20% margin would not be something to boast about. However, this owner knew that his overhead was covered and that this $2000 had no additional overhead burden. Therefore, the $2000 would just drop straight to the bottom line. Without that knowledge he might have walked away from the sale.

Elon Musk could probably run SpaceX or Tesla from his Bel Air home with a report from headquarters that detailed just 6-8 numbers. In Tesla's case some of those numbers might include number of cars produced, new orders, and any significant variations from budget lines.

Your company is no different. There are a very few numbers that you should want to see daily. Every company and situation is different, but think about what those numbers might be for you. Then make sure they are accurately gathered and presented daily or as often as you'd like to see them.

Step 10 - Make hard decisions quickly

During the course of a single day, any CEO is going to make hundreds of decisions. In fact, the tech community has now created a kind of rule about cutting down decisions. There is a reason why Musk and others are generally dressed the same every day, and the same as everyone else in tech…you know…black T-shirt and black jeans. Not having to make a decision about wardrobe each morning leaves more creative space in the soul for important decisions later on.

Musk has a very clearly thought out 6-step process for making decisions that is taught to all employees. This process helps to make even difficult decisions quickly but allows for making smaller decisions in less than five minutes.

I haven't been able to find a Musk quote regarding percentage chances of being right, He does say: "When something is important enough, you do it even if the odds are not in your favor." But Amazon CEO Jeff Bezos and others recommend 70% likelihood of correctness as the threshold. Here is the Elon Musk scientific method:

1. Ask a question.

2. Gather as much evidence as possible about it.

3. Develop axioms based on the evidence and try to assign a probability of truth to each one.

4. Draw a conclusion based on cogency in order to determine: Are these axioms correct, are they relevant, do they necessarily lead to this conclusion, and with what probability?

5. Attempt to disprove the conclusion. Seek refutation from others to further help break your conclusion.

6. If nobody can invalidate your conclusion, then you're probably right, but you're not certainly right. – Inc.

May I be so bold as to offer a 7th question. Is the decision reversible? If it isn't reversible, then the 70% threshold might need to be raised.

Chapter 8 – Asking Big Questions

In 2008, Elon Musk had his entire $190 million fortune riding on three companies, SpaceX, Tesla, and SolarCity (a separate company at that time.) Two of those companies were on the verge of failure. How much bigger does it get than the question he asked himself that day?

Should he allow one company to fail while trying to save the other? Should he allow both to fail? Should he try to save both with very limited resources and potentially have both fail? He chose the last option, which ended up working out very well.

Like Musk in this difficult moment, companies large and small, companies like yours, are commonly faced with existential issues. The difference between finding yourself locked out by your bank or your landlord or still having an opportunity to try another way often comes down to asking the right questions.

One company I know lost $250,000 two years ago, broke even last year, and seems destined to stay in that same position for 2019. Every effort to earn profits to improve seems stymied by lack of capital due to the losses in 2017. There is no money for promotion, R & D, etc. But the company has a set of attributes, including that the physical plant is underutilized, there is a trained staff, and the CEO has grit. What else could this company do with its attributes was the big question.

The possible answers were to use a second shift to do job shop work for other companies, produce some simple parts that are in demand that are not even related to the current product lines, add products not made that current customers would buy, sell the company to someone who had more financial reserves or access to more customers. By knowing the question, the owner was able to consider a string of options.

In another situation, a CEO looked me in the eye and asked, "Am I the right person to be running this company?" That's a big question. My answer was that she had the skill sets to do so, but she needed to execute better. What other possible questions or answers come to your mind in this situation?

Here are a few questions that qualify as big questions:

- Should I fire a large customer?
- Should I drop a major product or service?
- How much do I really care about increasing my income?
- What am I willing to sacrifice to see my company succeed?
- Why am I in business? This business?
- Who can I trust?
- Should I completely rethink my business plan? Processes? Staffing?
- What are the chances that this business will fail in the next year? Five years?
- Do I like working here?

You might turn to your staff, your customers, or your suppliers to help you determined the right questions. What are they seeing? Even better is to have a disinterested third party to brainstorm with. This could be a consultant, coach, CPA, board of directors, or a mastermind group.

Chapter 9 –
Rule Breaking Is Essential to Vision

True entrepreneurs are always rule breakers. Most business owners are somewhat proud of their view of rules as something to be challenged, disregarded, or even thrown out with great ceremony.

A common business rule that many young business people believe doesn't apply to their new enterprise is the law of margins. There is a widespread belief among many in their teens and twenties that businesses charge way too much for products and services and that prices are set high due to greed. If they could spend a few minutes looking over the financial statements of the companies I've consulted with, they would be shocked to see how "not greedy" most are.

Others are convinced that companies underpay their workers, should always give lavish benefits, and that the owners are slave masters who push their employees to the brink of exhaustion in pursuit of filthy lucre.

So, if you've been in business, you're laughing along with me here. However, check out a company called Costco. They sell products well under their competitors pricing, they pay their employees more, and provide good benefits. Profits are the result of charging annual dues and volume. Here we see our law of margins tossed overboard by someone (Sol Price) who broke the rules.

Elon Musk is the absolute king of rule breaking. When he entered the rocket business, every friend and confidant that he trusted told him not to do it. One such set of friends even compiled a video of rocket crashes to graphically convince him to find a more reasonable way to invest his

PayPal fortune. Sovereign nations with almost limitless capital and little restraint on time delays were quite capable of blowing up these machines and trashing untold billions of dollars.

How about Tesla? No new car company had succeeded in the US since Chrysler in 1926. Electric cars had been introduced by the largest car makers in the world, and the idea has failed. Even Musk says that he figured his chances of success were much less than 50%.

I doubt you can find a single expert in the field of maximizing employee production who will suggest pushing everyone to work 80-hour weeks while the boss works 100 consistently, month-after-month. Musk expects no less from his people.

Cars are transportation – right? No, they are technology products designed to move people and products from place to place. Rockets are one-use products – Duh! No, they should land on their butts like they do in science fiction movies and be reused. Distributed electric power is the only way to deliver low cost power to homes – everyone knows that? No, beautiful solar power roofs combined with battery packs allow homes to go off grid, or make money selling power back to the utilities.

This rule breaking mentality isn't just at the mission/vision level of thinking. It comes down to the shop floor. When you're building rockets, many of the parts have to be precision machined to tight tolerances, most often created for the precise purpose, and then manufactured in small quantities. This means that an item whose basic metal cost might be $2 could end up costing SpaceX $1000 or more when finally delivered.

Musk won't tolerate this type of thinking. His engineers and buyers commonly look for commercial equivalents to "rocket parts" and then prove that they meet the regulatory requirements with or without modification, which means that the part might cost $50 instead of $1000.

Of course, rule breaking can have a downside. Musk and Tesla recently had to cough up $20M each due to a bit of rule breaking that the SEC didn't find amusing.

Where might your company break some "rules"? During the heydays of the bicycle business most bike shops required that you leave your bicycle for a week or longer for repairs. That's how everyone does it. One shop decided to promise next day turn-around and improved utilization of their physical plant by having a repair team start at 6:00 a.m. They owned the repair business in their region, which also translated into more retail sales.

A barber friend was struggling until he started opening at 7:00 a.m. He found an entirely new demographic for his services. A restaurant gave away free meals the first weekend it was open and never had to advertise again. These companies broke with the everybody-does-it-this-way rules and customers flocked to their companies.

How might you break with the "it's always been done this way" mentality and create new customers, increase margins, or disrupt an entire industry?

Chapter 10 - Visionary

We have established that Elon Musk represents the type of entrepreneur we call visionaries. They have a canny ability to see the future. They may be totally wrong for any number of reasons, but their curiosity and analytic nature provides them with a strong sense of what will happen in the economy, the business world, and in the specific industry into which they hope to sell their products and services.

Visionaries can commonly imagine the specific ways in which they will produce, market, and fund their ideas, before they open their doors. Through this processing they separate the good ideas from the less good. Their rich imaginations can run through various potential versions of the plan, honing and sharpening each element of the plan. They see their own role in the plan, and they quickly realize where the biggest needs are.

It is possible that some of this process will require writing things on a napkin or working them out on a computer program, but a huge part of the vision-casting takes place totally in the mind.

Once the vision is concrete enough and a decision is made to float a trial balloon, this type of entrepreneur will seek the wise counsel of trusted associates. The goal is really to communicate, hone, rework, and sharpen the vision. When this process has proven fruitful, the next step is to work on a simple way of being able to show others the vision. If this part is done correctly, others will want to get on the bus. Partners, top level employees, and members of The Shark Tank will fully "get" the idea, and some will eagerly look for ways to benefit.

Once the business is actually established, the vision will be clearly articulated to staff and line employees to motivate and encourage them to excellence. They feel they are part of something bigger than life.

Obviously, you've seen this with Elon Musk. He borrowed the Apple method of doing big stage productions to introduce his ideas. Who wouldn't want to work for the guy who is trying to establish a colony on Mars or save the planet by forcing every car company in the world to switch to electric motors?

How might you reshape the way you do business in such a way as it incorporates your vision? Do you have a vision, or are you just trying your best to work by a recipe? Every company can gain from the formulation of a vision bigger than making a living. If you follow the above ideas regarding curiosity, analysis, and the rest, you should be able to formulate a vision for your firm.

Chapter 11 – Leadership – Musk Style

In reading *War and Peace*, I was primarily struck by one notion put forward by Tolstoy. He told the story of a soldier who was trying to figure out how to go home alive. He pointed out that on day one in actual battle, there is so much chaos that you basically try to survive. After some experience, you realize you probably aren't likely to survive, but you still think you have a chance. Thus, you strategize methods of upping your odds. No matter how much you work this approach, you are still terrified of dying in the field.

However, in order to be calm on the battlefield and consequently effective as a leader, you must consider yourself dead. You must accept that you can't get out alive. Now you are able to lead the charge and others will follow you.

This is exactly how it works in business. The owner/leader must appear to his troops to be willing to succeed or die trying. Jeff Bezos, CEO of Amazon, said that Amazon will die someday, and that his job is to keep it alive as long as possible.

The boss must be ready to do the hardest task that he asks anyone else to do. When the president does the dirtiest job in the building, it inspires folks to want to follow.

Musk is actually famous for his work ethic. He often works over 100 hours per week and rarely works fewer than 80. He commonly sleeps on an uncomfortable- looking couch in his office or on the factory floor. He tells the lowest paid workers that he wants to hear personally about issues that are affecting progress. Then he heads to the scene of the issue and participates in figuring out the solution.

Musk also puts it all on the line for the world to see. Again and again, he takes bold steps to go where no one has ever gone, and he does so in full view of anyone with the Internet. He says he will land rockets, tail first, and reuse the parts instead of dumping them into the ocean. Then he accomplishes the feat to the astonishment of the entire rocket industry.

He understood that his huge investment of time, money, and energy was on the line when his first three rockets failed at SpaceX, and there was only enough money left to try one more time. He went forward, and number four was a huge success. People want to follow leaders like that. Read the full story here: https://arstechnica.com/science/2018/09/inside-the-eight-desperate-weeks-that-saved-spacex-from-ruin/3/

When Musk messes up, he fesses up. This is another trait of great leaders. It also creates a reputation for transparency that helps when messes happen that aren't your fault.

What Can We All Learn from the Musk Leadership Style?

There are dozens of fabulous books on the subject of leadership, and one thing is evident from reading through these classics. No two have the same list of styles, practices, habits, or even personalities. Could there be two leaders whose approaches are more different that our 44th and 45th US Presidents? How about a comparison of Bill Gates and Steve Jobs? The goal of this section is not to suggest you become a carbon copy of Elon Musk in his approach to leadership. Rather, take from it what fits you and that you can grow from. Even if you pick only one of the following, and work on improving your capabilities in that single area, impressive gains are almost assured.

Vision

Thus far, a lot of ink has been devoted to the subject of vision; therefore, further comments will be brief. The best leaders have a clear vision for their ideas, their products, and their companies. They also understand that a leader without followers is a non-starter. So, consultants, suppliers, financiers, employees and customers must buy into the vision if the enterprise is to succeed.

Communication of the Vision

"Well, I try to make it a really fun place to work, really enjoyable. And I talk about the grand vision of SpaceX, where we wanna go, what we wanna do; we wanna take people to orbit and beyond. We ultimately want to be the company that makes a difference in extension of life beyond earth, which is one of the most important things that life itself could achieve. And so sort of you construct this great Holy Grail potential in the future. You have to stay grounded in the short term. 'Cause if you don't do things that pay the bills you're not gonna achieve the ultimate long-term objective. But it's nice to have that sort of Holy Grail long term potential out there as inspiration for coming to work," he said. - <u>Ladders</u>

There are literally thousands of products and companies that go into the dustbin of history because the leadership is incapable of communicating the vision.

Many years ago, I helped to introduce a product that was designed to keep bicycle tires from going flat. I was pretty certain that I had the rights to the golden goose. My customers, the distributors, confirmed my expectations and were willing to make huge commitments in order to be part of the success story. The retailers who had them in stock were doing a fine job of selling them to consumers. But our initial sales efforts plateaued well below our expectations.

My partner at the time, Terry Brown, found that many dealers were not stocking the product because they were horrified by what might happen. They had a robust repair business fixing flats and selling innertubes. They worried that this lost stream of income would undermine profits.

The communication of our vision was limited to talking about this miracle product that would stop 97% of flat tires. We had not communicated the benefits to a key component in our distribution chain, the dealer. In fact, the dealer found the product to potentially be a big detriment to his profits.

How would we communicate the vision to them in a way that it would get them to come on board. We started an advertising campaign that claimed flat tires were causing riders to hang up their bikes for good, and therefore never return to shops for any repairs, accessories, clothes, or upgrade bikes. Once retailers saw this connection, the results were almost immediate, and 35- years later, and I am still earning profits by selling a similar product under the name ThornBusters on Amazon.com.

Musk is a genius at communicating the vision. In fact, at one of the low points in the history of Tesla and SpaceX, Musk told his public relations staff that they needed to have something new to make headlines with every single week. Here was a vision within a vision. Get the company brand in the news week after week and build a continuous buzz around the progress of the products and the company.

Today, if you follow the news, you know that Musk himself, Tesla, SpaceX, or the Boring Company is in the news almost every single day, often many times per day. Public relations is one of the least expensive ways to communicate a vision, and Musk and company have brilliantly exploited this approach. The buzz excites every constituent you need to reach: buyers, suppliers, employees, prospective employees, fans, investors, bloggers, and even authors.

As a leader of a smaller organization that might not have quite the same access to the news, you can use email blasts, blogs, the company website, social media, and community involvement to make sure your vision is being communicated to those you want to hear it.

Second, your vision will be spread by your happy customers. Musk says he doesn't advertise at all because he knows his customers will tell their neighbors about their experience.

Is your staff trained to explain your vision to customers, suppliers, and their employees? What is it about your cakes, your tax service, your auto repair business that is worthy of your customer telling his neighbor? It needs to be evident in the quality of your products and services, the customer service, and is a specific and unforgettable take-away that helps the customer "pitch" you to friends.

Third, your vision will get a wide telling if you can get influencers on your side. Influencers are all the rage today, but I'm not so concerned about the paid influencers on social media. I'm really talking about the local radio host; the popular mayor of your town; the president of the PTA, chamber, or Rotary Club; the top enthusiast in your area for your type of product; and other professionals who share your client base. For instance, if you are a printer, have you explained your vision to every marketer in your area who influences printing purchases?

Passion

The term "passion" is almost always found on any list of leadership attributes. Though sometimes described as enthusiasm, energy, commitment, or positivity, the owner or manager who doesn't exhibit this characteristic is unlikely to wear the mantel of leader for long.

Consider this question that I often ask salespeople: If you are not excited about yourself, the company you work for, and the product you sell, why on earth would you expect the prospect to be excited about you, your product, or your company?

This is even more true of the leader who must be as passionate as the sales person talking to a prospect. Additionally, that enthusiasm must be clearly evident when a leader is talking with bankers, suppliers, and prospective employees.

Musk is often perceived as having a hesitant speaking style during TED talks or in interview settings. Like so many technical types, he tends to be extremely careful about selecting each word, and his delivery is not smooth. But there is no denying his enthusiasm or his vision when he speaks. You believe that he believes, and his almost boyish charm makes you want to believe what is often truly unbelievable. As a result, his TED talks and videos have a huge following.

No one would ever call his presentations scripted, but when you listen to videos of interviews, you find that he is saying many of the exact same sentences, years, or even decades, apart. Over a dozen years after he first announced that he wants to die on Mars, although not on impact, you still understand his emotional commitment regarding colonizing Mars when he speaks today.

When you talk about your vision, your products, and your company, do listeners catch your passion, or do you come across as tired, bored, robotic? What about your employees, especially sellers and buyers? I can't tell you how many sales people I've had the unpleasant chore of listening to who were not passionate. (Owners, too.) But almost worse than an unenthusiastic sales person is a bored buyer. Suppliers are more important than customers because there are many, many more customers than good suppliers. Therefore, it is imperative that you make sure you and your staff understand the importance of romancing suppliers and their personnel with the passion of your undertaking.

Leading the Charge

I hate stating the obvious, but the fact that leaders must be out front would seem to be an absolute like almost no other. To my way of thinking, President Obama made a serious misstatement about leadership that we can only hope will have no resonance with future leaders. He suggested that the US would lead from behind. I kept waiting for the President to give some explanation for what that meant or where he'd learned such a thing.

If you Google the idea, you'll find that this was an idea championed by Nelson Mandela. If you are currently following the horrific results of Mandela's leadership in the destruction of South Africa, then you need no other reason to reject this notion.

You will never see Elon Musk leading from behind. Musk is out front and exposing his jugular in every way imaginable. He makes bold statements, he accepts responsibility for falling short on those statements, he works harder and longer than anyone in the company, and he's willing to subject himself to any difficult task or hardship that he'd ask his people to do.

Do you have a reputation for being out front taking flack, or do you hide in your office when the unhappy customer comes in demanding a refund and becomes belligerent with your staff? Are you only too happy to go on the road with your sales reps or would you prefer to stay home and revise a spreadsheet? Do you work every day of a trade show or go to the bar halfway through the second day like most of the owners?

Can you be a successful leader from the safety of your office? Maybe, but it is very unlikely.

Servant's Heart

How do you really feel about your customers? Your employees? Your suppliers? I am constantly amazed when I hear owners talking about all three in disparaging ways, especially when these are the three groups without which they would not be making a living.

Musk gets the concept of a servant's heart:

> *Musk made the 2017 Glassdoor Highest Rated CEOs list and defined how he thinks of leadership in an interview with the company this year.*

> *"Your title makes you a manager, but your people make you a leader. We want our leaders to find ways of motivating and inspiring their teams, reduce the noise in their work and help remove blockers. If you are a manager or leading at any level at SpaceX, we stress that your team is not there to serve you. You are there to serve your team and help them do the best possible job for the company. This applies to me most of all. Leaders are also expected to work harder than those who report to them and always make sure that their needs are taken care of before yours, thus leading by example," he told the site. -* **9 of the best Elon Musk secrets for success.** By: Jane Burnett

Great leaders care about people. Elon Musk has been criticized for some of his treatment of employees. I hope to be able to ask him directly about this, someday. I'm going to guess that he'll feel that companies and employees are often mismatched, and that if an employee is not fitting into the culture, that employee will be better off when they find a culture they can fit into.

On the other hand, Musk has a reputation for having a cult-like following among his employees. Some of these folks have felt his wrath, but sometimes it is necessary to get tough on a soldier in order to prepare them for the fight in a way that is most likely to get them through unscathed. Do you care enough about your people to be straight up with them about where they are missing the mark?

Recently, there was some news attention suggesting that workplace injuries in Musk's companies were a concern that wasn't being addressed. Musk put out a memo saying that every injury must come to his personal attention. Here was his email:

> "No words can express how much I care about your safety and wellbeing. It breaks my heart when someone is injured building cars and trying their best to make Tesla successful."

> "Going forward, I've asked that every injury be reported directly to me, without exception. I'm meeting with the safety team every week and would like to meet with every injured person as soon as they are well, so that I can understand from them exactly what we need to do to make it better. I will then go down to the production line and perform the same task that they perform."

> "This is what all managers at Tesla should do as a matter of course. At Tesla, we lead from the front line, not from some safe and comfortable ivory tower. Leaders must always put their team's safety above their own."

And then there is this from his second wife:

> He doesn't have to listen to anything that doesn't fit his worldview. But he proved he would take shit from me. He said "let me listen to her and figure these things out" he proved that he valued my opinion on things in life and was willing to listen. I thought it was quite a telling thing for the man – that he made the effort. – Elon Musk: Tesla, SpaceX and the Quest for a Fantastic Future by Ashlee Vance

Delegation

There are three levels of delegation that a leader MUST learn and teach if they are to be successful: delegation of the job, delegation of the responsibility for the job or for the people under their supervision, and delegation of the authority to act on the leader's behalf.

It goes without saying that you can't micromanage a business with 51,000 employees, although if Musk could be slighted on any leadership skill, it might be this one.

Most leaders fail to delegate because they don't trust their staffer, because they can do it better and faster than the employee, and/or because they become impatient with the pace of the work.

As with everything in this book, I'm basing my conclusions on the public record, and that record would seem to expose a leader who sometimes takes back the delegated task and does it himself, and who sometimes ignores the chain of command and takes an action that undermines the responsibility or the authority of a manager regarding some aspect of their job.

Without making excuses for Musk, this likely arises because he continues to be very hands-on in the details of the development of the products and systems necessary to execute his plan and on or near his timetables. He creates crazy expectations and then won't take "no" for an answer. When someone says "no," or has no solution to offer, he may take action against that employee directly, thereby undermining the managers.

If you want a business to grow, you must delegate. As a general rule, you can manage up to 9 people without delegating any responsibility or authority. After that, your organization will become more and more inefficient if you keep trying to manage all of the work. Most such owners are also likely to take back some of the actual tasks that have been delegated, further eroding efficiency.

Once you reach 25 or more employees, you'll need to start delegating authority. This is the hardest step. How are you doing with delegation? I find that this is one of the most likely barriers to successfully growing a company.

Follow Through

Great leaders would rather die than disappoint. This is often the reason a leader will interfere in delegated matters. Someone will be disappointed, and the leader will feel horrible.

Of course, there are going to be times when any human will disappoint constituents. The evidence that everything that could be done was done will then be the measure used by loyal followers. How the leader responds to a failure will have a massive impact on how the followers will react.

In 2018, the financial press watched intently as Tesla attempted to deliver on the promise of producing 5000 model 3 cars per week by the end of the second quarter. As the deadline approached, Musk kept trying different approaches to get to his goal. Reports had him working 120-hour weeks, sleeping on the factory floor, and admitting that Tesla had underestimated the importance of humans in production of the Model 3. Then Musk brought in a massive tent and created a new assembly line under the tent.

Musk and his team did achieve the goal, but the attention from the news media and the consequent publicity was worth so much more than the actual result. The optic was clear. Tesla and Musk are innovators, hugely committed, and passionate about what they do. Fans, workers, stockholders, and many who had no real connection to the man or the company, cheered him on.

Are you seen as the kind of leader who can be counted on to follow through? Do you show up early to appointments, keep your commitments, own your misses, and do you show dogged determination during the darkest hours? When you do, others will be in your corner.

Integrity

Many of the other items on the list of leadership traits are issues of integrity, but there are some specific earmarks associated with this characteristic that require a separate list.

Long before there was a #MeToo movement, there was a group called Promise Keepers. While the primary goal of Promise Keepers was to emphasize the kind of integrity that husbands and dads need to exercise regarding their families, the teachings offered by this group went much further.

The Promise Keepers organization proposed that managers never have a closed door when a member of the opposite sex is in the office. They proposed that two individuals of the opposite sex not drive long distances to business events together or go to restaurants together. The idea was that even the perception of an inappropriate relationship was to be discouraged.

Musk has been called out a few times on the issue of integrity regarding some business decisions. Without giving him a pass, these instances would appear to be the exception rather than the rule. And in a few cases, he has been able to show pretty conclusively that the reality was far different than what his detractors suggested.

Growing up I often heard that a reputation was hard to build and almost impossible to recover once lost. If those you lead feel you are lacking in integrity, they may believe that they have license to follow suit.

Are you keeping two sets of books; pocketing cash payments and not reporting that income? Are you paying some employees under the table? If you get an over-shipment or an incorrect invoice in your favor, do you take advantage of your supplier? Do you cut corners on quality where you think you can get away with it? Do you pad hours when you invoice services?

Your employees are watching. I worked for a company that purchased a retailer. The owner of the retail business sealed the deal by proudly showing our owner his safety deposit box full of hundred-dollar bills. This was his off-books income. After taking over the business, we noticed a major drop in profits. After some sleuthing, we realized that the employees knew about the cash skimming, and they had copied the methods to their own advantage.

You may see short term advantages from acts lacking in integrity or pushing into gray areas. Great leaders are generally those who are trusted by those they lead.

Chapter 12 –
Goal Setting

"Shoot for the moon. Even if you miss, you'll land among the stars."
Norman Vincent Peale.

If you haven't read *The Power of Positive Thinking*, by Dr. Peale, you have missed one of the classics on motivational thinking. Add it to your must-read list. He wasn't the first to make this admonition or something similar to it, but his version probably had the widest audience. Elon Musk certainly has been one who has given the concept specific and practical application.

Ray Dalio says, "What you think is attainable is just a function of what you know at the moment," Remember that great expectations create great capabilities. If you limit your goals to what you know you can achieve, you are setting the bar way too low."

Musk is nothing if not aspirational. He is mocked, scorned, and ridiculed for his crazy ideas and his proclamations of intentions to do the seeming impossible. Then he is constantly harangued by his detractors for falling short or being later than promised, even as he changes entire industries and accomplishes feats heretofore only contemplated by sovereign states.

A few of his current goals:

- Begin to land material on Mars for a future human colony in 2022
- Send humans to Mars in 2024
- Make and sell 1,000,000 electric cars per year
- Create high speed transportation in tunnels in Chicago and LA by 2020.
- Build 20 Gigafactories

These are just a few of his major goals, but you see, a goal without a strategy is just a dream. In the case of Elon Musk, the goals are filled with strategies with goals for the execution of each strategy followed by levels of such goals and strategies down to "Can you have the sun visor problem figured out by Friday?"

Musk would be the first to admit that he is often very optimistic on his timetables. His promises, for instance, to deliver the first Tesla Roadster, the S, the X, and the 3 were all off by months or even years. But he dares to set goals, really BIG goals that no one else is even contemplating.

There are huge advantages to setting aspirational goals, especially those that go beyond mere sales and profits.

> *"It's better to approach this [building a company] from the standpoint of saying–rather than you want to be an entrepreneur or you want to make money–**what are some useful things that you do that you wish existed in the world?**"* Elon Musk quoted in High Existence

My primary goal for this book is to provide business people with some practical steps for finding greater success in their enterprises. It is easier to get folks around me excited about *that* goal than if I were to declare that I hope to sell a million books and buy a beach house on Maui.

And yet, profit is important. Musk understands the obvious; without profit, your company ultimately fails. But he also sees profit as a way of measuring the value of your enterprise:

> *"I think the profit motive is a good one if the rules of an industry are properly set up. There is nothing fundamentally wrong with profit. In fact, profit just means that people are paying you more for whatever you're doing that you're spending to create it. That's a good thing."*- Trendlee

Musk's huge goals only include saving the world and creating an escape hatch from earth in case we humans end up really screwing things up here. Some would call him crazy, but others are willing to write him large checks, make introductions, buy his products, and work crazy hours in harsh conditions to help him make these dreams into reality.

From a TED Talk with Chris Anderson

CA: "Why, Elon? Why do we need to build a city on Mars?"

Elon: "I think it's important to have a future that is inspiring and appealing…I just think there have to be a reasons that you get up in the morning and you want to live. Like, why do you want to live? What's the point? What inspires you? What do you love about the future? And if we're not out there, if the future does not include being out there among the stars and being a multiplanet species. I find that it's incredibly depressing if that's not the future that we're going to have."

This can be true for the smallest business. I am consulting with a small company in Eugene Oregon that makes fold up bicycles. The owners and employees of Bike Friday believe they are doing their part in the battle to move humans away from a carbon-based economy. The owners have not gotten rich from their 25 years in business, but they have thousands of fans who are enthusiastically helping them to hit their goal.

Goals don't have to be lofty to be important and motivating. In fact, many goals may be clearly mercenary.

The history of Tesla is filled with such goals. When the Model S was introduced, a perfect storm of problems threatened to put the company into bankruptcy. Many reservation holders were not converting into buyers. Musk quickly put together a salesforce made up of folks who didn't normally wear that hat. He told them to get on the phones and sell or there would be no company. His goal was to save the company. His strategy was to call in the cavalry. You may have already guessed the outcome. This makeshift, rag tag sales force, saved the day.

Musk has had clear goals for himself since college, and maybe even before. He knew that he wanted to make a difference, not just do a job. I can remember that many of my college associates had similar goals. Somehow, over the years, some of those big dreams were either dashed or forgotten for many. One thing is clear – it is never too late.

Look at the slate of presidential contenders for 2020. Many are all in their '70's. Whether they are truly hoping to do good for the benefit of America and Americans or have other motives, they do have some very serious goals that they are pursuing at a time when many are chasing golf balls.

The best goal setting begins with clarity. What is your purpose? As Musk asks, "What inspires you?" Maybe you are inspired by material gain. Musk hopes you can afford a Tesla. Maybe you are not that interested in material things, but you are getting a bit grey in the temples, and you'd like to have a decent nest egg. Maybe the kids are nearing college age and need some tuition money, but repaying college loans are not a part of your perfect plan.

On the other hand, you might want to save the world or your little corner of it. Over the years I have had a range of goals, including ending flat tires on bicycles so that more folks would ride, creating the first bicycle water bottle that didn't leak, and helping entrepreneurs realize their business purpose. For most of us, these goals are more inspiring than financial goals, but the financial goals are often critical to making the other goals.

Musk says over and over that he must make a profit in order to do the good he has as his ultimate purpose. The very profitable rocket business creates the very seed money for the Mars project. If SpaceX doesn't make billions of dollars taking other people's stuff into space, then there won't be any way to purchase or build the needed equipment or money to send pioneers to Mars.

The more clarity we have about our ultimate purpose, the easier it is to start breaking down the strategies and subordinate goals to get there. With Tesla, Musk's goal is to shift the thinking of major auto companies to make electric cars instead of internal combustion engine (ICE) cars. He has often said that he doesn't even care if Tesla survives, as long as the auto industry shifts to sustainable energy.

But, in order to force that shift, in order to get monolithic corporations with huge fixed capital and investments in ICE to spend billions on electric, he has to show that the public will buy electric cars. The track record for electric cars in 2002 was not very good. While the big auto makers were messing around with hybrids and electrics, they weren't going all in.

Musk knows history, and he knows that car companies often start out making expensive toys for adults. He believes that if he can make a perfect car, not a nice car that happens to be electric, but a perfect car, then it won't matter how it is propelled. If the energy source is electric power many potential buyers will see that as a plus. But the perfect car must be stylish, fast, equipped with creature comforts and provide a value proposition. Musk has set his goal to make the perfect car. How's that for a lofty goal? And this is just his sub-goal under the greater purpose of changing the world by changing the fuel source of choice for autos.

The strategy looks like this. Make a roadster that makes money. Use that success to raise more money and make an expensive sedan that can make money with moderate sales. Use that success to raise even more money to eventually create an electric car for the masses. Eventually, build one-million cars per year. Somewhere in this process the other makers will determine that they are missing the shift in consumer sentiment and will start seriously investing in all electric vehicles.

What if you were an accounting company, a CPA firm. Most folks would say that an accounting business is about as boring as can be, and they question how anyone could disrupt that industry. What if your goal as a CPA went way beyond helping companies compile their financials and save on taxes? What if your goal was to help American businesses become much more successful? What if you believed that if small and medium sized businesses became more successful, it would help the economy so much that the least successful among us would have a huge chance at financial security? What if you further believed that this idea would be exportable and that you could raise the standard of living around the entire planet through better accounting?

Insert your potential world changing mission into the formula. Would you be more eager to get up in the morning if you were going to disrupt your industry rather than just pay the bills?

Chapter 13 – Networking Is a Core Value

"Join a group that is amazing that you really respect or if you are building a company you've got to gather great people." Elon Musk – Get2Growth

The world has gone through a dramatic shift over the past 25 years. The Internet and smart phone have definitely changed the way people interact. We are less social in this time of social media. And the younger generations are less social than the previous generations. This reality has created an opportunity that is ripe for exploitation. Those who are willing to reach out socially and find ways to connect and create community are building successful networks.

While we may all be amazed by the creative intellect, the outlandish goal setting, and the mindboggling products put out by the Musk enterprises, what may be lost from view is his networking skills and the critical component that employees play in his businesses. (We'll deal with the employees in the next chapter.)

If you read the Musk biography, *Elon Musk: Tesla, SpaceX, and the Quest for a Fantastic Future,* I'm confident you will come away with a totally different view of Musk than his portrayal in the rest of the press. I believe that he would agree with me that without his network and his talented staff, none of his hopes and dreams would have been realized.

Musk has had partners from the very beginning. Often his partners were family members, but also friends he made in college or in various groups he was part of. In addition to his actual business partners, he developed large networks of associates that could and did help him with resources, necessary connections, financing, and emotional support.

This brings to mind the greatest US industrialist at the turn of another century, Andrew Carnegie. Carnegie was the wealthiest man of his era and credited his people:

> *"Take away my people but leave my factories and soon grass will grow on the factory floors......Take away my factories but leave my people and soon we will have a new and better factory."* - Andrew Carnegie

Carnegie would later challenge Napoleon Hill to interview other industrialists of his age to see what they all had in common. Hill was able to get in front of Edison, Ford, and others. One of his conclusions was that each of these men had done what Carnegie described this way:

> *"We have here in this business a master mind. It is not my mind, and it is not the mind of any other man on my staff, but the sum total of all these minds that I have gathered around me that constitute a master mind in the steel business.*

> *"I have been many years gathering these men around me and building this mind. Each man contributes an important part to the building of this mind. I do not always agree with all the men on my staff, on all matters, nor do they always agree with me.*

> *"Perhaps some of us do not like each other from a personal viewpoint, but I know that I need these men and they know that they need me in the maintenance of this master mind that is necessary in carrying on this steel business."* **Napolean Hill** in Think and Grow Rich

> Hill concluded that, *"No two minds ever come together without thereby creating a third, invisible intangible force, which may be likened to a third mind."*

As Musk continued to build his various companies, his network grew to encompass many household names in technology. The talent at PayPal came to be known as the PayPal Mafia. There is no way to make this point more clearly that to post a list of the members of the Pay Pal Mafia from Wikipedia:

- Peter Thiel, PayPal founder and former chief executive officer who is sometimes referred to as the "don" of the PayPal Mafia[5]
- Max Levchin, Founder and chief technology officer at PayPal sometimes called the "consigliere" of the PayPal Mafia[4][12]
- Elon Musk, is founder of X.com which acquired the company Confinity. Musk later co-founded Tesla Motors, SpaceX, OpenAI, The Boring Company, and is the Chairman of SolarCity[3] [8][13]
- David O. Sacks, former PayPal COO who later founded Geni. com and Yammer[3]
- Scott Banister, former Ironport CTO and PayPal board member[14]
- Roelof Botha, former PayPal CFO who later became a partner of venture capital firm Sequoia Capital[15]
- Steve Chen, former PayPal engineer who co-founded YouTube. [16]
- David Gausebeck, former PayPal Technical Architect, co-creator of the Gausebeck-Levchin test, co-founder of Matterport Inc., a digital 3-D modeling company. [17]
- Reid Hoffman, former executive vice president who later founded LinkedIn and was an early investor in Facebook, Aviary,[18] Friendster, Six Apart, Zynga, IronPort, Flickr, Digg, Grockit, Ping.fm, Nanosolar, Care.com, Knewton, Kongregate, Last.fm, Ning, and Technorati[3][19][20]
- Ken Howery, former PayPal CFO who became a partner at Founders Fund[21]
- Chad Hurley, former PayPal web designer who co-founded YouTube[8]
- Eric M. Jackson, who wrote the book *The PayPal Wars* and became chief executive officer of WND Books and co-founded CapLinked.[22]
- Jawed Karim, former PayPal engineer who co-founded YouTube. [15]
- Rod D. Martin, former special counsel to CEO Peter Thiel whose 10X Capital took over Galectin Therapeutics in 2009 and who founded Advanced Search Laboratories in 2012.[23]

- Dave McClure, a former PayPal marketing director, a super angel investor for start up companies[24] and founder of 500 Startups which has hit 500+ investments. [25]
- Andrew McCormack, co-founder of Valar Ventures [26][15]
- Ken Miller, original vice president of risk management at PayPal, and is now a venture capitalist at Omidyar Network as well as an original board advisor to Square and Eric Jackson's company, CapLinked.
- Luke Nosek, PayPal co-founder and former vice president of marketing and strategy, became a partner at Founders Fund with Peter Thiel and Ken Howery[27]
- Jason Portnoy, former vice president of financial planning and analysis who later became CFO at Peter Thiel's Clarium Capital, CFO at Palantir Technologies, and founding partner at Subtraction Capital.
- Keith Rabois, a former executive at PayPal who later worked at LinkedIn, Slide, Square, and currently Khosla Ventures, and personally invested in Tokbox, Xoom, Slide, LinkedIn, Geni, Room 9 Entertainment, YouTube, and Yelp.[15]
- Jack Selby, former vice president of corporate and international development at PayPal who co-founded Clarium Capital with Peter Thiel, later becoming managing director of Grandmaster Capital Management.[28]
- Premal Shah, former product manager at PayPal, became the founding president of Kiva.org.[4]
- Russel Simmons, former PayPal engineer who co-founded Yelp Inc.[15]
- Jeremy Stoppelman, former vice president of technology at PayPal who later co-founded Yelp, Inc.[3][5][7][29][30]
- Yishan Wong, a former engineering manager at PayPal, later worked at Facebook and became the CEO of Reddit.[31]

Imagine having this list of individuals in your data base and just a phone call or text away. Have you built your own mastermind group to help guide you, encourage you, and hold you accountable?

I feel so strongly about this approach to business building and career success that I started a company to help business people come together in mastermind environments.

Why did people of this caliber establish business relationships and friendships with Musk? It seems safe to say that they were impressed by the vision, the intensity, and the scope of enterprise. There have been thousands of others along the way who didn't get it, didn't care, or thought Musk was crazy. They didn't last long in the growing Musk universe.

But it was Musk's cold calling that added many of these names to his data base of friends, customers, suppliers, employees, advisors, and investors. Jim Cantrell received one of those phone calls while he was driving in his convertible. He recalls that he could barely hear Musk over the wind noise and because Musk spoke so fast. But that phone call put Cantrell into a tight -knit inner-circle that provided Musk with his early education on rocketry. Cantrell even loaned Musk four of his textbooks. When it came to these cold calls by Musk, Cantrell had this to say in a CNBC Interview:

> *Cantrell said he's heard Musk's elevator pitch so often he is still able to recite the speech from memory, more than a decade later:*
>
> *"I'm Elon Musk, I'm an internet billionaire, I founded PayPal and X.com. I sold X.com to Compaq for 165 million dollars in cash and I could spend the rest of my life on a beach drinking Mai Tais, but I decided that humanity needs to become a multi-planetary species to survive and I want to do something with my money to show that humanity can do that and I need Russian rockets and that's why I'm calling you."* How Elon Musk's cold calls to rocket scientists helped kickstart SpaceX - Published Tue, Aug 28 2018 • 8:30 AM EDT • Updated Tue, Aug 28 2018 • 10:08 AM EDT - CNBC

It would also appear that Musk built the relationships based on the honest desire to listen to their expertise and/or because he was willing to offer them something they needed with no expectation of getting something back.

That should be true for each of us. If we have an exciting vision and can communicate it with passion and clarity, there will be those who will want to follow or at least be associated with you because of your vision. If we build relationships based on giving rather than getting, that will cement the deal.

Who did Musk seek out? He says that, at first, he was looking for knowledge and skill, but later he came to realize that character mattered more:

> *"The biggest mistake in general that I've made—and I'm trying to correct for that—is to put too much of a weighting on somebody's talent and not enough on their personality [...]. It actually matters whether somebody has a good heart. It really does. And I've made the mistake of thinking that sometimes it's just about the brain."* – <u>High Existence</u>

Who should you and I seek out? I'd say that Musk's criteria are solid. He looks for people with character and talent. Three of the most talented people that have ever been in my circle of associates were clearly dishonest, but not in overt ways. I knew this in every case, but I dismissed their lack of character because of their talent. In each case they eventually tried to undermine me and my business.

How to Network Effectively

It would appear that Musk had a base of techie friends that he met at university. They had similar world views and enjoyed the same kinds of diversions. He would later strategically join certain clubs or loose-knit groups that offered cohesive groups of say...hobbyists who liked to build rockets or electric cars.

In the bicycle business (where I spent most of my professional life), many of the really successful companies grew out of groups of similar hobbyists who liked to fix up their bikes to do something new, like race downhill on dirt pathways at breakneck speeds or jump twenty-inch bikes off ramps and do flips.

Where are the hobbyists meeting in your industry? Who is crusading or organizing or innovating? Find those folks or be one of them. Be a giver of your time, energy, enthusiasm, evangelism, and talent. Be an absorber of their excitement, ideas, vision, and then apply all of this to your own business. Musk did this over and over in every business.

Fearless Networking

Alert – You won't like this section! 'Want to change your business and your life? Get over yourself! Stop letting your pride get in the way of your success. Doors don't open by themselves, you have to walk through them and be okay with a "no."

Until he was in his twenties, Musk is described almost universally as a shy young man, and few saw any evidence of his future potential. But shy or not, Musk was not shy about asking for help, orders, financing, partnerships, or affiliations.

The buyer at Walmart is probably less educated and paid less than you. Why should you fear him or any other buyer? The banker you need to approach for a loan is probably more fearful of losing his job because of not making quotas than you are of asking for a loan. Fear of making these kinds of calls is a success killer.

Participating in networking events can be hugely helpful in building a business, but I know plenty of owners and salespeople who are profoundly intimidated by attending these affairs. It is the same kind of fear of rejection that stops folks from making cold calls or from following up on a call to find out if the buying decision has been made.

After reading about Musk, it would appear he had no such trepidations. In his early twenties, he was approaching major newspapers to sell them his idea for internet advertising of local businesses. In his thirties, he was calling on Russian government officials with the goal of buying an ICBM.

If you'd like to learn more about how to Network, I'd point you to *When Friday Isn't Payday*, available on Amazon at bit.ly/WFIP_3

Chapter 14 –
Valuing All Human
Resources

"All a company is, is a group of people that are gathered together to create a product or service. So, depending upon how talented and hardworking that group is, and the degree to which they're focused cohesively in a good direction, that will determine the success of the company. So, do everything you can to gather great people if you're creating a company." Elon Musk – <u>Simple Thing Called Life</u>

As of November of 2019, SpaceX and Tesla combined employ 52,000 people.

Leaders need someone to lead, and selecting the right people is a huge component of success in any business. My lifelong mantra has been to hire the best and let them do their job. Musk appears to feel the same.

"I want to accentuate the philosophy that I have with companies in the startup phase, which is a sort of 'special forces' approach. The minimum passing grade is excellent. That's the way I believe startup companies need to be if they're ultimately going to be large and successful companies. We'd adhered to that to some degree, but we'd strayed from that path in a few places. That doesn't mean the people that we let go on that basis would be considered bad–it's just the difference between Special Forces and regular Army. If you're going to get through a really tough environment and ultimately grow the company to something significant, you have to have a very high level of dedication and talent throughout the organization." Elon Musk - <u>High Existence</u>

In the previous chapter on Networking, we sited the famed statement by industrialist Andrew Carnegie regarding how critical his people were. Clearly Carnegie was primarily speaking about his top tier of leaders and managers. However, that type of attitude filters down the chain of command. If the CEO is known to only hire top people, it is very likely that his second shift supervisor knows this and hires with a similar style. And if not, that second shift supervisor will likely get the boot.

Musk has been known to call professors and deans with the express goal of finding the top recruits that meet his criteria.

> *Musk would personally reach out to the aerospace departments of top colleges and inquire about the students who'd finished with the best marks on their exams. It was not unusual for him to call the students in their dorm rooms and recruit them over the phone. "I thought it was a prank call," said Michael Colonno, who heard from Musk while attending Stanford, "I did not believe for a minute that he had a rocket company." Elon Musk: Tesla, SpaceX, and the Quest for a Fantastic Future*

Would that work for you? As this book is being written, there is a massive shortage of labor in the US with unemployment at historical lows. Many business owners count finding qualified people as the most difficult task they face in the current environment. If recruiting talent in their dorm rooms wouldn't work for you, what other creative methods might?

> *The space X hiring model places some emphasis on getting top marks at top schools, but most of the attention goes towards spotting engineers who exhibit type A personality traits over the course of their lives. The company's recruiters look for people who might excel at robot building competitions or who are car-racing hobbyists who have built usual vehicles. The object is to find individuals who ooze passion, can work well as part of a team, and have real world experience bending metal. "Even if you're someone who writes code for your job you need to understand how mechanical things work," said dolly Singh, who spent five years as the head of talent acquisition at space X. "We were looking for people that have been building things since they were little."*

Sometimes these people walk through the front door. Other times, Singh relied on a handful of enterprising techniques to find them. She became famous for trolling through academic papers to find engineers with very specific skills, cold calling researchers at labs and plucking possessed engineers out of college. At tradeshows and conferences, SpaceX recruiters wooed interesting candidates they had spotted, with a cloak and dagger shtick. They would hand out black envelopes that contained invitations to meet at a specific time and place, usually a bar or restaurant near the event, for an initial interview. The candidates that showed up discovered they were among only a handful of people who would been anointed out of all the conference attendees. They were immediately made to feel special and inspired. Elon Musk: Tesla, SpaceX, and the Quest for a Fantastic Future

I have written extensively about a far more mundane but patently successful method using temp-to-hire through local agencies as an inexpensive way to get top-notch people. You pay an extra cost for 90 days, but you have almost no cost of acquisition other than clearly explaining to the agency what qualities and skill sets you seek. This is no need for posting job notices, wading through applications, calling and setting appointments, mind-numbing interviews, fear of future lawsuits from asking wrong questions, or calling disappointed candidates. Need I say more.

Musk has never been shy about recruiting top prospects from his competitors. He has found many top people who are willing to work harder and for less immediate income in order to be part of a vibrant future-oriented company rather than a staid old-school company.

There is a dark side to the Musk method – His churn rate on employees is very high. This is due to a number of reasons:

- Musk doesn't suffer fools gladly – He seems very quick to fire those who aren't measuring up
- Musk insists that employees have a solution when they present a problem – failure on this issue can be a firing offense
- Musk doesn't ever want to hear that something "can't be done."

- These startup companies have had ups and downs, and with that comes lay-offs.
- Many employees burn out due to VERY long work weeks and the constant pressure to produce at very high levels.
- Musk doesn't seem to be good at passing out kudos for success.

So, why do so many employees stay? Primarily because it is motivating and exciting to work towards cutting edge, world changing, solutions. How many workers are tuning in to a streaming channel once or twice a month to watch a rocket they helped to build, launched into space, and then see those rockets performing feats that no rocket has ever done before.

Many people are at their best and happiest when being pushed to the max. Four or five years at Tesla or SpaceX is likely to produce huge dividends for future employment due to experience, connections, and knowledge gained during that time. In many ways, working for a Musk company is like earning an advanced degree.

Jim Cantrell says it this way in a Quora answer Oct 20, 2014

> *"I was only around SpaceX in the early days, but I am guessing that the process has not varied widely. It starts with who is hired. ALL of our early hires had to talk to the founders and Elon. They had to all like them and generally came as personal references from existing employees. There was a lot of credibility to be lost by recommending someone bad. I recommended Gwynne to replace me when I left since I had known her for a long time. She has obviously proven out well. So, I would have to say that the creative process is more focused on assembling the right team than any other magic. The team has to be focused on the same priorities and has to be the brightest out there. Elon insisted on that. **I think that the creativity that comes from the right mixture of people co-located is almost defacto something that happens. They challenge each other, add to ideas, offer different perspectives.**"*

When I was making and printing bicycle water bottles, a mundane business compared to rockets and electric cars by any measure, we set the quality standard for our industry. We had to press hard on our entire staff to improve every step in the process in order to achieve the goal of being the best. Employees were exceedingly proud to be known as the best printers in the business. You can create this type of environment in your business if you choose to.

.

Chapter 15 –
Executing on the Vision

Lots of people have ideas. They even have outstanding ideas. Some of these folks create some kind of plan. They may make drawings, apply for patents, look for funding, consider locations, talk to vendors, or even draw up an elaborate business plan and form a company. There are those who do all of the above and make some product, call on some customers, set up a store (online or off), or do some kind of promotion in an attempt to sell their idea.

In my career, I have commonly been known in my industry as someone to take ideas to. This was especially true in the bicycle industry. During the go-go years of the bike biz, plenty of garage tinkerers and even sophisticated individuals were pretty sure they would make their fortune selling bike stuff. I have many stories. Most of these ideas fail because the person with the idea has no ideas how to execute, lacks the funds to execute, or is unwilling to do the hard things to execute.

When you wake up in the morning, and contemplate your day, you have some conscious and even more unconscious ideas about what you can execute. You can cook breakfast, drive kids around to school and soccer practice, do a good enough job at work to keep getting a paycheck, and maintain friendships, family connections, and such. You are probably very able to execute Facebook or Instagram and maybe an assortment of games on your various devices.

When you woke up this morning, did you, in your wildest imagination, think you could run for governor of your state? How about opening a car repair business? Would you feel that if you worked pretty hard at it, you could become a brain surgeon in ten years or so?

The vast majority of us not only have some idea about what we can execute, we also have some ideas about what we cannot. It is this author's contention that the difference between mature adults and those who are not is the clear understanding of what one is capable of and what is sadly off the list of potential future accomplishments.

I can't draw a stick figure that folks can identify. I'm okay with that. But I'm a decent enough writer. I played some pretty good baseball, but failed miserably at bowling, even after years of effort. I ended up being a manufacturer with 25,000 square feet of blow molders and printing equipment. There is no way I would have planned to do that, but every step of the way I knew I could take the next step and execute.

Elon Musk wakes up in the morning and believes he can create rocket ships and electric cars and tunnels under Chicago and neural transmitters from computers to our brains. If I told my wife that I believed I could do those things, I suspect she'd have me visit the shrink. If I set out to do something that bold, I'm pretty sure I'd fail miserably.

Elon Musk actually executes his wild and crazy ideas. I really want to interview him, someday, to determine if executing the creation of the largest factory under one roof in the world is for him the equivalent of writing a book for me. He just knows he can do it?! I think that's the case.

Stating the obvious; if you can't execute your idea, you need to give it to someone who can. You need to be mature enough to know your limitations, and yet believe in yourself enough to stretch in areas where you do feel competent. One way to get some clarity on these decisions is through a mastermind group. There is an entire section devoted to having a group of trusted advisors elsewhere in the online portion of *When Friday Isn't Payday*. Click here

Musk also says that he didn't really want to become a rocket scientist, but he couldn't find someone to hire who understood his vision. So, he was forced to do it himself or abandon the plan. Like Musk, you may find that you don't have certain skill sets, and you need to hire for those. You might also get a partner for some of those. You might also be able to find a vendor to take care of some things you can't do.

Chapter 16 – Risk Taking

Is this chapter necessary?! As noted in the introduction, Elon Musk is very, very unique. I don't aspire to be him, and he will even tell you that you shouldn't hope your children turn out to be him. But could you be 1/100th as effective at the tasks in this book as he is?

According to Forbes, Musk is worth at least $21B. That would be over $10B for Tesla and another $10B for SpaceX. So, if you worked at 1% of Musk's efficiency you could be worth $210,000,000 by age 47. Ok. How about just 1/1000th – Your worth $21,000,000. Is that you? Drop it down to 1/10,000th. Maybe you are worth $2,100,000, so that without ever working again, your annuity for that amount is providing you with at least $120,000 a year.

Let's take an inventory. You are probably 75% as smart as Musk. You might be more educated. He only has two BS degrees. But let's say you are only 50% as educated since you have a two-year degree. I'm going to say that you are only 1% as well read. He has probably read 100 books a year his entire life. But haven't you read at least one per year?

What about pedigree. He has a very good family history. Lots of smart, talented, pretty, people. However, his childhood was wracked by bullying, divorce, and an abusive father. So maybe you had troubles in your early years and your pedigree is not so impressive. Would you agree you had at least a 25% as good a head start in life?

Consider Musk's financial status as of age 20, which was at $0. So, you might have him beat on this one.

So why is Musk worth $21B and you're not? Up until now, you've hopefully been inspired to up your game in some very simple ways. Hire better, network better, be more curious, set goals, have a vision, become a better leader. I would speculate that if you improved 5% at just those six things, you'd dramatically improve your income, personal success, and enjoyment of both your business and personal life. But then there are the big ones. And what is bigger than risk.

I tell my kids that there are three things that determine how much money you make. Are you willing and able to manage things and people? Are you a good salesperson and willing to sell? Are you willing to take risks?

If you are in business for yourself, you clearly have at least some appetite for risk. You've been willing to risk lower income, potential failure, and some amount of time, energy, emotion, and your fortune on your business.

But if you had made a few hundred million dollars, would you turn around and invest every penny in a rocket company startup, an electric car startup, and a solar panel startup? Would you be so all in that you would not be willing to sacrifice one to improve the chances of the other? Would you also be willing to risk substantial amounts of other people's money? Would you then work 100-hour weeks for as long as necessary to make sure you squeezed every last drop of your capability into insuring success?

Me neither! No way. Now that we have that out of the way, the real question to ask is: How much risk are you willing to take in order to achieve a particular reward?

When hiring salespeople, I have a standard set of offers. I start by asking them the minimum amount they need to earn so that they will not worry about their electricity being cut off? Let's say the answer is $2500 a month. I explain that I don't want them to be so desperate for rent money that the desperation is oozing out of their pores during a presentation.

I suggest that I have two alternative approaches to paying sales people. One method pays a base of $2500 a month and a 5% commission. The other method gives a $2500 draw and a 10% commission, which starts with dollar one.

In the second case, the sales person needs to hit $25,000 in order to "earn" the base and would earn less than method one until $50,000 in sales. However, after $50,000, the second approach pays far better.

Which would you take? If you take door #1, you are risk averse. If you take door #2, you are risk perverse; that is, you like a bit of risk in your life.

Now this test is not going to separate the Elon Musks of this world from you and me. But it is a starting point for assessing your current feelings about risk. Possibly if you turned to me after the offer and said, "I'll take 15% and no base or draw, that would move you along the continuum. You could even go further and state that if you don't sell at least $25,000 by the third month, you'd return all commissions earned for having wasted the companies time.

There were hundreds of investors and employees in the Musk enterprises who love that kind of risk, but there was also the promise of a huge payoff, and that's the other side of the risk equation.

I would not risk $100,000, work 60-hour weeks, and spend endless amounts of emotional equity in a business where I'd be satisfied with $75,000 a year. But I have personal relationships with dozens if not hundreds of owners who have made huge investments of time, energy, and actual cash for incomes that are in that range. In many cases, risking more would yield big returns, but the appetite is no longer there. The income covers their personal expenses at an acceptable level, so the risk of pain or loss is too great compared with what is seen as an elusive or uncertain potential gain.

Does that mean that everyone in that position should hang their head in shame? Absolutely not. They have succeeded to build a business that is providing a sustained income for them and their family. It is not a character flaw to draw back from risk at that level or twice that level of income. However, a clear understanding of where you are on the risk continuum will help you make decisions about how much to rely on risk-taking compared to other ways to grow your business.

Chapter 17 - Overcoming Obstacles

"Starting a company is like eating glass and staring into the abyss."

"That's generally what happens," explains Musk. "Because, when you first start a company, there's lots of optimism. And things are great. Happiness at first is high. And then you encounter all sorts of issues--and happiness will steadily decline. Then, you'll go through a whole world of hurt. And, eventually, if you succeed--and in most cases you will not succeed ... And Tesla almost didn't succeed. It came very close to failure. If you succeed, then after a long time, you will finally get back to happiness."

This is so true. When I started working for myself several years ago, I wasn't prepared for the amount of pain I'd have to endure. And I've failed more often than I've succeeded.

But every failure was a lesson learned--and the successes wouldn't have been possible without them. Elon Musk – Inc.

This chapter could be a book unto itself. In the early days of Tesla, a supplier explained that changing a door was harder than changing an engine.

He <Ian Wright> was shocked when a Lotus engineer told him that it was easier to redesign an engine than remake a door. In what would become a theme for Tesla, seemingly simple parts revealed unending intricacies. You have to fit locks, switches, and windows into the confines of a door, all while keeping rain and wind out and getting that satisfying thunk *when you close it. Perhaps most maddeningly, a would-be carmaker has to navigate manufacturing tolerances. – Business Insider*

The early Tesla team was trying to build a totally new car, but they were counting on Lotus to merely change an existing car to fit their purpose. They knew that they would have to make huge changes to the chassis in order to support the batteries, but soon learned just how hard it was to create a new car.

Now contemplate that this was one of the easier obstacles that Musk would need to overcome in his almost 30 years of building companies, products, and services.

What is the starting point for a company policy regarding overcoming obstacles? I will offer just three, and they are right out of the mouth of Elon Musk.

Musk begins by looking at the possibility of success. For him it is an equation arrived at through the scientific method and his six steps to making a decision. Once the decision is made, then there is an assumption that the task will be completed, for as you now know, Musk never gives up.

However, there are many, many obstacles to overcome in building a new car or rocket, not to mention attaching the human brain to your computer. So here are the three approaches I promised:

> *...be ready in case it doesn't work out. It's easier to recover from a failure if you already have a backup plan. – Elon Musk -* Forbes

There are plenty of success books available that will tell you exactly the opposite, that if you have a plan B it works against plan A. I agree with Musk. In fact, in *When Friday Isn't Payday*, I give a lengthy description of a method which uses three- track thinking. I can't prove it, but suspect that Musk often has a plan C to go along with plan A & B.

Musk is certainly not the first to offer the following advice:

> *"Failure is an option here. If things are not failing, you are not innovating enough."- Elon Musk -* Forbes

This is a core of entrepreneurial thinking. Always be looking for improvements in every aspect of the business. Keep a completely open mind and a willingness to try new things. Musk goes on to say that:

"Some people don't like change, but you need to embrace change if the alternative is disaster." – Elon Musk - <u>Brainyquote</u>

If your organization is overly resistant to change, (all organizations are at least somewhat change averse), then you may need to make changes in your organization.

Third in the admonitions regarding overcoming obstacles is an iconic Musk statement that needs no further comment:

"You should take the approach that you're wrong. Your goal is to be less wrong." *– Elon Musk –* <u>Inc.</u>

Chapter 18 – Creating Quality

I'm going to give you a very odd definition of quality – "whatever you decide it is."

Dollar Stores has built a massive company through the sales of low "quality" items. Two Buck Chuck would never be called a "quality" wine. All "B" movies grade themselves. The road to success is not about whether you are making the best widget. It is about whether you are making your widget the best in class and meeting or exceeding your own specifications.

Your customer does not always need "the best." They may be a value shopper, or they may prefer to buy the cheapest and throw it away when it stops functioning. Ikea has built a huge business around the idea of purchasing furniture you can just throw away when you change your interior design approach.

However, what if your IKEA products were always missing parts, chipped, or the instructions made no sense (Yes, it's true, they do get away with horrible instructions.) If IKEA's quality was not at the level expected for the price, then they would start to lose customers.

Musk is generally shooting for that other definition of quality, which is **the best possible quality and performance with no compromise allowed**. This is a great position to occupy in the marketplace. In general, I would always prefer to be the top quality/top price or the lowest price. The middle often gets squeezed.

The buyer of a $50,000 car expects quality at every turn, and Musk knows this, expects it from his troops, and is relentless in making the changes when flaws are brought to his intention. Every single part of the car is poured over for ways to improve style, function, fit, and detail.

> *Musk sank into the model S driver seat and von Holzhausen climbed in the passenger seat. Musk eyes darted around for a few moments and then settled on to the sun visor. It was beige and a visible seem ran around the edge and pushed the fabric out. "It's fish-lipped," Musk said. The screws attaching the visor to the car were visible as well and musk insisted that every time he saw them it felt like tiny daggers were stabbing him in the eyes. The whole situation was unacceptable. "We have to decide what is the best sun visor in the world and then do it better," Musk said. A couple of assistants taking notes outside of the car jotted this down.* <u>Elon Musk: Tesla, SpaceX, and the Quest for a Fantastic Future</u>

If quality matters to you in your business, you will need to communicate this as part of your overall vision. It must be baked into every aspect of the business. There must be plenty of carrots and sticks that remind every member of the team that you esteem quality. Quality results should be pointed out publicly with high praise. Failures must be dealt with quickly and as privately as possible. Employees must understand that the ultimate "stick" of being let go is always on the table.

Many owners make the mistake of allowing poor quality because of the assumed cost. You need better equipment, better people, more training, quality control processes, and sometimes lower productivity to achieve more quality. But W. Edwards Deming and Philip Crosby have proven beyond doubt that quality is at least free and might be a profit center for some companies. The cost benefits include: less rework, less scrap, less downtime, fewer returns, easier to sell into all sales channels, increased brand approval, more and better WOM (word of mouth), and better morale in your entire organization.

Musk suggests yet another reason to push for unparalleled quality:

> *"A lot of companies get confused; they spend money on things that don't actually make the product better. For example, at Tesla, we've never spent any money on advertising. We put all the money into R&D and manufacturing and design to try to make the car as good*

as possible. I think that's the way to go. For any given company, keep thinking about 'Are these efforts that people are spending, are they resulting in a better product or service?' And if they're not, stop those efforts." - <u>Curiosity</u>

What would you be willing to pay for a headline that describes the quality of your product as requiring an adjustment in the methods of judging quality? This is what *Consumer Reports* said of the model S as it awarded it a perfect score. The correct answer is "priceless." How about a headline in February 2019 that voted the model 3 as the car that "brings the most joy."

And what would be the cost of having other headlines complain that the fit and finish on body panels are not up to what owners of $50,000 vehicles expect? When that headline hit regarding the Model 3, Musk pushed the pedal to the metal in both fixing the issue, but also drowning out the negative headline with a steady stream of the positive. Even after spending those resources, you can bet that the majority of prospects for Tesla vehicles will now be "aware" of the issue as they make a decision between a Tesla and the dozens of electric cars that are coming to showrooms near you.

Your company may not have the kind of press coverage Tesla gets for every nuance of their hits and misses, but your products, services, customer service, and image all send messages to your customer. In what ways might you up your game to provide better quality?

Chapter 19 –
Insists on Incremental Improvement

"So, there's really two main dimensions along which cost optimization and making something available in the national market can be achieved. One is design iteration, going through multiple versions of something, and then the other is economies of scale. You kind of need both of those things in order to make compelling mass market product. If you look at, like, cell phones and how many design iterations have we gone through with cell phones and look at the scale at which they are made, which is enormous; and that's what enables everyone to have a supercomputer in their pocket." <u>Video of Code Conference 2016</u>

Have you ever done the math on incremental improvement? Craig Korotko, my partner in SoCal MasterMinds does a fantastic seminar as part of his business coaching. Craig owns a FocalPoint Business Coaching franchise, a Brian Tracy product. Through FocalPoint Craig has been trained specifically in the concept of incremental improvements.

Many business owners who are pushing hard trying to grow their business only look at the top line and put huge amounts of effort into growing sales. And to be sure, there are stages in the business growth cycle when that is really critical, such as at startup.

However, as important as sales are to any enterprise, sales don't buy the steaks. Profit, or even more exactly, free cash flow is the only thing that really improves your personal income. Free cash flow is a combination of many moving parts in your business: Sales, margins, overhead, capital needs, shrinkage, and more. Breaking things down further, margins are a combination of price and cost, overhead has fixed and variable expenses. Within those two, there are many line items, and all of these have an effect on free cash flow.

So, let's say you want to increase your personal take home by 30%. You might estimate that a 30% increase in sales would accomplish that result, give or take. For the purposes of this experiment, we'll assume that to be true.

Sales 30,000
Cost of sales $15,000
Overhead $10,000
Profit $5000

30% Increase in sales

Sales 39,000
Cost of sales 17,700
Overhead 11,200
Profit $6,500

What would happen if you had a 10% increase in sales, a 10% decrease in cost of Goods (based on the larger sales number) and a 10% decrease in overhead (also based on the larger sales number)

Sales $33,000
Cost of sales, $15,930 (90% of $17,700)
Overhead $10,180 (90% of $11,200)
Profit $6,890

You see, by paying attention to the other components, you were able to achieve a greater take home with less sales increase. Can you always find another 10% reduction in overhead or cost of goods? Maybe; maybe not. But consider that each and every line item might give you better results than only going for more sales.

Musk hammers on incremental improvement. You can watch almost any interview where he gets into the weeds about the manufacturing side of things, and he will soon get to the speed of throughput, the best use of humans vs. robots, and the ways that quality can be improved. Here is

<u>one video</u> you might enjoy in the Tesla factory. Musk variously discusses: how a current turntable that turns the car around as it is handed from one robot to another can be eliminated if they can figure out how to have the car go directly from one robot to another; the pace of the assembly line for the model 3 being .6 mph during that video (Aug 2018), where the model S is up to 1 mph; and how a single bolt in a single location could be the bottleneck to increase in throughput.

Musk is well known for walking through a factory, noticing some item that catches his well-trained eye, and starting a conversation with employees about first principles regarding that part, and how improvements might be made, or costs lowered.

Making incremental improvements can apply to every aspect of your business and personal life. Athletes know this and train to shave parts of a second off their time. Business coaches work hard to help their clients become more efficient users of their time, incrementally freeing up time for higher priority, best use of time functions.

Imagine if you were to make five, 3% improvements in your personal efficiency and performance, and another twenty, 3% improvements in various processes, procedures, pricing, and costs throughout your business. The grand total might be far more take home than a 30% increase in sales.

A great starting place is to look at every expenditure, every process, every customer, every employee and ask the most basic question of all, "Is this _____contributing to my bottom line?" Then start asking that question about any potential new expenditure, employee, etc.

We've seen members of our MasterMind groups jettison employees, customers, product lines, suppliers, and locations due to the recognition that these pieces were actually having a negative effect on the overall performance of the company.

As this is being written in January, 2019, SpaceX and Tesla have each announced large workforce reductions even as they ramp up for higher sales. As difficult as this may be*, **the market has little sympathy for inefficiency.***

Chapter 20 - Relentlessness - Passion Plus Persistence

"What does 'super hard' mean? [...] Work hard like, every waking hour. That's the thing I would say, particularly if you're starting a company. If you do simple math, say somebody else is working 50 hours and you're working 100, you'll get twice as much done in the course of a year as the other company." Elon Musk - <u>Curiosity</u>

Most small businesses do not require passion to reach some small level of income. A lawyer or doctor can open an office and with a bit of managerial skill, they'll make a living. You can say the same thing about many skilled workers who own businesses based on their ability to deliver a skill or make a decent product.

The entrepreneur isn't interested in the income. She isn't interested in a nice business that pays the bills. The goal is not about money, fame, or success. It is about the vision. Success is helping people live longer or better, creating life altering opportunities, offering adventure to those who love to try new things, finding a new way to lower the cost of producing something so that more folks can afford it.

"Notice that money is not an ingredient in any of these factors nor is intelligence. Admittedly, higher intelligence makes some fields (maybe rockets for example) easier to learn but by and large these ingredients are never a major factor in success. If you combine these three elements into your pursuits in life, you will be very successful, and the money will come on its own. Money is a reflection of the true value that you are creating.

How does this relate to Elon? When he came to me in 2001, he knew nothing of rockets or space exploration, but he was deeply passionate about it. In fact, he was so passionate about the need to 'make humanity a multi-planetary species' that he was willing to spend a very large portion of his fortune on it. But because he was intelligent, he knew that he needed rockets to launch probes into space. To prolong his money supply, he needed to buy the cheapest rockets available. Hence his interest in Russian launch vehicles. Once he understood the space market a bit better, he saw that there was also an enormous opportunity to disrupt the launch vehicle market. He was thus led to the conclusion that his time and money might be better spent 'solving the launch problem' as he put it back then than 'throwing away my fortune in some Russian warehouse'.

SpaceX was born after Elon spent some time with John Garvey (a co-founder of my new company Vector) who was building amature liquid launch vehicles in his garage at the time. While this seemed like an insane endeavor and John's neighbors worried about him, Elon saw the brilliance in it and decided that John's small rockets were an existence proof of something much bigger. Elon knew that if a small band of Space Cowboys like John could build a 30 foot tall liquid rocket with left over beer money and regular machine tools, great things were possible with big money, a great team and lots of hard work. This is where SpaceX was born.

SpaceX was not an obvious success in the early days. Clearly Elon and the team he recruited were passionate about building a low-cost launcher. Clearly, we were good at it. And clearly there was a market. However, most of the world was betting against Elon from the outside. This skepticism was born of a bit of conceit on the part of the big aerospace concerns who thought that 'nobody can do better than us and especially not a band of Space Cowboys like SpaceX'. There were also questions of Elon's motivations and basic honesty brought up by the skeptics. Others in the industry confided in me at the time that they thought Elon was fundamentally dishonest and making promises that he couldn't keep.

I left SpaceX after about a year because I too doubted SpaceX's ability to succeed with the amount of money they had raised (and I could not conceive of raising more). I also did not share Elon's passion for colonizing Mars as I regarded it to be a fool's errand as it would never happen in my lifetime. I was wrong on both counts. Elon did succeed in the end and it was because he never counted himself out. He never gave up. He kept going. He knew that he had the three ingredients and he kept upping the ante every time that he faced an obstacle or failure.

This leads me to what I personally think is the most important personal attribute for success. It's not intelligence. It's not being educated. It's not even experience. It's simply a determination to never ever give up. That is the most important element of success: dogged determination. One of my favorite quotes along these lines is from Garth Stein, author of the book Racing in the Rain.

'A winner, a champion, will accept his fate. He will continue with his wheels in the dirt. He will do his best to maintain his line and gradually get himself back on the track when it is safe to do so. Yes, he loses a few places in the race. Yes, he is at a disadvantage. But he is a winner, a champion, and will accept his fate. He is still racing. He is still alive'" Jim Cantrell - September 29, 2018 Quora answer

In 2016, Musk did not need another company, product, or venture after all his other successes and so much on his plate. But he became passionate about the potential to take the freeway systems subterranean. He knew he could execute. He bought a used tunneling machine and started playing around with it. Once he had his vision, he started talking to mayors and governors and even the President about changing our cities for the better. Are you passionate enough about your product to start calling on those who will benefit? Will you keep calling on those folks even after you have 20 or 30 people turn you down?

Everyone talks about Musk's *relentlessness.*

Dave Lyons, co-founder, Peloton Technology, former director of engineering at Tesla: "In December 2007, four of us flew across the country to Detroit to triage where we were on the transmission.

This was a period of time when he was absolutely stretched to his limit, and he saw all of his stuff in massive jeopardy. I've got to paraphrase this, but here goes: 'I've spent all my money and all of my friendships on this. It has to succeed. You need to do whatever is possible to make this happen — you need to use special forces methods to make this transmission happen.' I watched in his eyes that night how incredibly invested this guy was. I have never seen anybody in my life who was willing to put everything on the table the way I saw him that night." What's Driving Elon Musk

Over and over, Ashlee Vance gives gripping accounts of Musk sleeping on the office floor, working over 100 hours week after week, cheering on the troops after disasters, investing his own money when it seemed utterly foolish, and risking entire companies on the next launch of a rocket or a product.

As we get close to the end of this odyssey, let's take a reality check again. Very few business owners are this relentless and persistent, because very few have a goal beyond how much money they are going to earn. When the reason for owning a business is to make a paycheck, you become less inclined to take risks, and more inclined to guard your gains.

However, you might have a combination of goals concerning your enterprise. There may be many different aspects of what you do that energize and motivate you to take risks and work harder than anyone else, and that list might include a certain income. So, there is a middle ground. What can you learn from Elon Musk's persistence and take-no-prisoners approach that would work for your company? How can you teach it to others?

Of course, there is a breed of entrepreneurs who privilege the product far more than its earning power. The object might be as pedestrian as seeing a new product or company succeed, or it might be as outside-the-box as colonizing Mars. For these entrepreneurs, the end game is worth the risk. Falling short can be seen as failure, and failure is not an option, even if it is a likely outcome. If that sentence seems odd to you, think about it deeply because it is central to the entire story of Elon Musk and, perhaps, to your story.

"Starting and growing a business is as much about the innovation, drive, and determination of the people behind it as the product they sell." Elon Musk — <u>Inc.</u>

"Persistence is very important. You should not give up unless you are forced to give up." Elon Musk - <u>LifeHacks</u>

***"I don't ever give up. I'd have to be dead or completely incapacitated."** –* <u>**Elon Musk Quotes**</u>

Conclusion

I am no Elon Musk. You probably aren't either. I think I've said that before, at least once. But here's the critical part. You don't need to be an entrepreneur like Musk or even meet the pure definition of a visionary entrepreneur that I proposed in the introduction in order to be a successful business person. Not in the least. The insights here were written for ALL small businesses.

In order for you to succeed at the highest possible level, the goals you set must be those that match your passion, your personality, and your definition of success. Having said that, many owners I know haven't taken the time or spent the emotional currency to identify their own passions, much less defined what success looks like to them. These are steps Musk has clearly undertaken that anybody can do if they are willing.

The real purpose of this book is to give you some insight into yourself. Identifying what makes you tick and developing some of the attributes described here will benefit any business and potentially drive your profits much higher. They will also improve the quality of your life. Those two reasons might be reason enough to incorporate Musk's principles.

If this book has been helpful, I'd like to suggest some other materials that could be of use. Twenty-five years ago, I wrote _When Friday Isn't Payday._ It has stood the test of time and was just released in a third updated version. In this work you will find an A-Z business Bible that gives an overview of almost every aspect of running a business. It starts with a series of questions every entrepreneur should ask before opening a new business or even a new division. The book takes the CEO through the opening, the growth years, and into maturity. It closes out with recommendations and approaches to selling or otherwise transitioning the company when the owner is ready to retire.

Recently it was recommended that I also divide *When Friday Isn't Payday* into two shorter books. *Launch and Grow Rich* is the first half and deals with planning and opening a new business.

Give Yourself a Raise is the second half. This book is designed for companies that are growing and/or are in the mature phases.

I have created a website that contains many shorter articles that provide deeper dives into various subjects designed to help your business become more successful. Several of these are also short versions of books that will be released later this year. One of these books is *Finding Hidden Diamonds in Your Financial Statements*, co-authored with CPA, Shaila Chamberlain. The goal of this book will be to help owners who do not have a background in accounting to learn methods of seeing opportunities for improvements in sales, profits, and processes merely be setting up financial statements properly, then learning to read them.

As I have noted in the body of this book, my passion right now is opening MasterMind groups. I encourage every owner to either start such a group, join a local group that is already active, or join one of mine. You can learn more at https://SoCalMasterMinds.com. At this time, all of our groups that meet in person are located in the Inland Empire area of Southern California. We have also just decided to test an online version.

I would definitely like to encourage anyone reading this book to reach out through email at RandyKirk77@gmail.com. I would love to hear how you have benefited from this journey. through the life and approaches of Elon Musk. And, taking a page from his approach, I'd also love to hear your criticisms and suggestions for improvements. I can promise you that criticisms without solutions will not gain much traction. That is a Randy Kirk method.

Why do so many companies fail?

Why are so many owners stuck with low income and ROI? What would it take to turn most of these companies around?

Doing the Hard Things

Discover the 29 things you should be doing to increase your income and skyrocket your success!

This eBook is not available for purchase, go to authorremake.com/hard-things to get this exclusive guide now.

Made in the USA
Middletown, DE
19 January 2020